WRITING
with
Moxie

How to add the sparkle and banish boring

HOLLY CARDAMONE

Cover design, internal design and typesetting: Kerry Cooke, eggplant communications

To those with moxie – let's share it with the world

Table of Contents

CHAPTER SIX:

Introduction

Few writers rely on pure natural talent. Even fewer are able to bang out something that's perfect on their first go. No changes required. Hit publish! That's not to say there aren't some supremely talented writers out there scribbling away. I'm constantly blown away by people's ability to weave words. That doesn't discount the fact that the act of writing is actually a craft, and like any craft, requires dedicated practice, experience, and skill. This is a message I don't believed is shared enough. Nobody would expect a builder to 'whip up a house' off gut feel. There's plans, expertise, knowledge and of course, a practical toolkit, both metaphorical and literal, to move from bare ground to mock-Georgian McMonstrosity. So too with writing! Just as there's timber, steel, nails, plasterboard and, presumably, bricks and mortar, (that's the extent of my building knowledge) there are many approaches, frameworks, strategies and structures that elevate words on a page to language that truly connects and compels. Writing with moxie, if you will.

My goal with this book is to share tips, exercises, techniques and real examples to get you writing, and then get you writing *better.* I'm aiming for practical—I'd love you to read a tip, then go and apply that learning against your own writing, be it cleaning up a social media caption or completely rewriting an 'About' page to make it more *you*.

Chapter One

WHY WRITE BETTER?

The power of storytelling lies in connection. From connection we have impact and, at the very least, entertainment in the truest sense of the word.

> '*At any given moment, all around the world, hundreds of millions of people will be engaged in what is one of the most familiar of all forms of human activity. In one way or another, they will have their attention focused on one of those strange sequences of mental images which we call a story.*'
>
> ~ Christopher Booker

With improved writing, we're better placed to hold the attention of our readers. We're more interesting, captivating and compelling. Our brand begins to do the heavy lifting of confirming and clarifying who we are and what we do. As we connect with others we can change behaviour through the intentional way we string letters and words together to craft a message that we want our readers to receive.

So, what does it mean to write better? What sets good writers apart from the merely average?

SO, WHY THIS BOOK?

In 2020 I wrote a little somethin'-somethin'. To be specific, I wrote 189 pages of somethin'-somethin' that became my book, *Tell Your Story - build your brand and grow your business*. My intention for *Tell Your Story* was to help people step into the role of communications director for their brand and/or their business. I wanted to share clear information to help people create a plan of attack to communicate effectively with their audience. I encouraged readers to approach their communications like a writer, supported with a hefty dose of strategy to take advantage of the incredible opportunity that storytelling offers people to build their brands, personal or professional profiles and everything in between.

The feedback was next level. You know that meme that says, "When you buy from a small business there's an actual person doing a happy dance?" That was me. With every review, with every email, with every comment or DM from people who had read my book and found something great to action, I performed what can only be described as a Highland Fling—probably not by actual Scottish Highlanders. They'd find it offensive.

But, but, but... Now, here's the thing: I like big butts and I cannot lie.

People were buying my book, reading my book, taking action from my book, but there was a disconnect. At the workshops I was delivering, in my messages, in responses to my emails and in my one-on-one work with clients, I was hearing that the actual craft of writing as a medium for sharing a message was a stumbling block for many, many people.

> *'Skill is how you close the gap between what you can see in your mind's eye and what you can produce; the more skill you have, the more sophisticated and accomplished your ideas can be.'*
>
> ~ Twyla Tharp

As a writing mentor, every day I watch accomplished, formidable people fight internal battles and question their writing ability, either overtly or through sneaky, insidious acts of self-sabotage that, frankly, limit their ability to get out of their own way and connect with people through their writing. What a horrible loss for them, for their potential audience, for the broader world! And yes, that feels a tad dramatic, even for me. I'm no psychologist, so the mindset stuff I can't really help with, other than telling that mean inner editor to bugger off.

The craft stuff? That I know. That I can help with. And guess what? Nail that and the mindset wobbles tend to take care of themselves, or at least abate enough to STFU and allow you to get on with things. When you feel armed with writing skills and knowledge, you'll be equipped to add the sparkle to a chunk of writing to make it decidedly non-boring and manage your time to enable a writing habit which reinforces and consolidates those skills.

Chapter One

MY STORY

For as long as I can remember, I've wanted to be a writer. Year after year, when asked what I wanted to be when I grew up, my response never changed: writer.

I wrote all the time—when I was a wee thing it was poems on little scraps of paper (Mum still has them, in her sock drawer of all places!) diaries and short stories. As I grew older, my writing became journals, novellas, song lyrics and poetry that makes grown up Holly want to reach through time to give teenage Holly a good slappin', a hug and sometimes a combination of both.

When I wasn't writing, I was reading anything and everything I could get my hands on. There was the obligatory Enid Blyton, alongside *Trixie Belden* and *Sweet Valley High* (I *know*, shutupshutupshutup). One summer holiday, when I must have been under 10, I read a couple of *Bobbsey Twins* books that I found in the (creepy AF) bungalow at my grandmother's house, long abandoned and out of print, even then. I knew the librarian at my country town's library by name, which makes it all the more baffling that at the age of around thirteen she allowed me to borrow *Wifey*, Judy Blume's first novel that was decidedly NOT for children. There was a lot of random crap in my reading lists, no doubt about it, but it was offset by Quality Literature with a capital Q. I was blessed with incredible English teachers who constantly handed me books they thought would inspire, challenge, or provoke me, or that basically I'd enjoy. I remember in Year 10 reading a novel under the desk, opting out of the class discussion on the literary devices behind a memoir—*Tracks* by Robyn Davidson, if you're interested. (I loathed it as a fifteen-year-old but loved when I reread it in my early forties. Riddle me that!) My teacher walked past, suggested not unkindly to not be so disrespectful, and she followed it up with the comment, "Great book, come see me when you're finished because the ending destroyed me; I want to know what you think." How amazing is that?

I entered HSC/VCE with my eyes firmly set on English and English Literature subjects, setting me up for a career that involved writing in some way, shape or form. I was thinking author, but with a back-up plan along the lines of journalism, advertising, PR, publishing and editing. I even had a PR work experience placement working for a government department. I was so excited, yet understandably daunted to be leaving the farm and my beautiful high school cocoon where I felt nurtured, seen and heard, to spend a week pouring myself a cup of ambition in Melbourne's CBD. The placement spiel detailed events and launches, Ministerial speeches, potentially even the opportunity to meet the Premier. On my very first morning, my 'supervisor' asked me what skills I could bring to the PR team, and, in one of the greatest facepalm moments of my life, I stupidly confessed to being able to touch type. For the next four and a half days, I sat at the sole computer monitor on the entire floor, tasked with taking hard copy documents and turning them into electronic files, letter by letter, word by word, sentence by sentence, paragraph by excruciatingly boring paragraph. The kicker? It wasn't even anything remotely PR-worthy or inspired. It was HR policy and procedure manuals. Inspiring stuff. I didn't leave the floor and I certainly didn't meet the Premier. Not then, anyway. That surly sixteen-year-old who resentfully typed from 9 am to 5.30 pm, thinking of how to make most creative use of the $25 paid for five days of work would go on to write for three Premiers of Victoria, including her favourite, the Honourable Joan Kirner. *swooning at the very memory*

I smashed Year 12 English and English Literature. I had my heart set on an Arts degree and pursuing my writing dream. My careers counsellor, on the other hand? She was a fan of a pragmatic back-up plan and steered me towards a health sciences degree. I baulked. She also made mention of the fact that the better writers leaned on their life experience, and as a private school girl who'd grown up on a farm, let's face it, I had very little. She showed me the potential career paths, the guaranteed income (people are always going to get sick, after all), the stories I'd have access to of people at their most vulnerable and the ability to have something to 'fall back on.' The night before the university selections were due I caved, and applied for Nursing at Monash University. Life experience, come at me!

Next came four years of following a path I knew wasn't destined for. The first sign? My first assignment was an analysis of a doctor-turned-patient's memoir with the not-so-hidden message about how dehumanising the health sector can be to the end recipients. After achieving High Distinction HSC English Literature results I thought I had this in the bag. Apparently not. I was told in no uncertain terms that I couldn't write. This was followed by another barely passable grade when I couldn't bring myself to wax lyrical about the writing of a certain much-heralded grief expert. Ugh. That first year of nursing really did a number on me—I left Year 12 being someone who wrote constantly, across many genres and forms. I then didn't write anything even remotely creative for ten years, and it was a hole in my life that, without exaggeration, ached.

The second sign I followed the wrong path? My level of pride or even baseline interest in my degree was so non-existent that I didn't bother graduating. I had my degree mailed to me. I saw no point in a graduation ceremony. I did my time, I did the 'right' thing by having something to fall back on, and so now it was time to actually fall back on nursing. I trotted back to university.

While I was 'retraining' in communications, I did Saturday night duty shifts across Melbourne while doing communications temp work. I wrote in *Tell Your Story* about the stars aligning for me when my temp recruitment agency was tasked with the seemingly impossible task of finding someone who had communications skills plus nursing experience. I teamed up with a project specialist who had worked on some of the most transformational campaigns in Victoria. She became an incredible mentor, and I was in the enviable position of having a phenomenal agency to work with to bring a multimillion dollar campaign to life. It was the kind of work experience that money can't buy, and I lapped up every lesson that came my way. There were some interesting moments—I had been involved in medical emergencies and life-threatening crises, but hadn't experienced the pressure that came with saying, "Sorry Minister, I'll write that policy announcement speech in the morning. I have to get to my *Globalisation's impact on poetic form in the era of cyberspace* class."

By night, I was learning the theoretical framework behind best practice communications and writing for different mediums. By day, I was putting all that theory into practice, embedding and consolidating theoretical concepts into communications I could see, feel, and touch—communications that connected our audience to the message. I saw first-hand the impact of incredible communications—we took a state-wide shortfall of public sector nurses of around 1,200 to one of excess, while shifting the public perception of this one-of-a-kind profession. Communications (and story-based comms at that) turned a jaded workforce from one that was demoralised and feeling undervalued (because, let's face it, they were) to one whose professionalism was given the spotlight. I was caught, hook, line and sinker. Story-led communications for the win!

I'd found a way to bring writing to my professional life beyond nursing care notes that included swathes of description such as 'dirty old man' and 'petrified faecal matter lodged in umbilical crevice.' And yes, you're welcome for that last visual. I wrote one hell of a thesis exposing the dangers of online health information; how very prophetic of me, long before 2020's pandemic paranoia. The very same day I had my graduation ceremony for my Master of Communications, I enrolled in a Master of Arts in Writing and Literature program. Finally, finally, FINALLY, I was deeply immersed in the world of writing: poetry, literature, fiction and creative non-fiction. Ever the pragmatist, I also threw in an editing unit to upskill myself in that area, realising I'd been misusing em dashes my entire life. Oh, the horror!

From here, I started a side hustle, Holly Cardamone Communications and Freelance Writing, later rebranded as Blue51 Communications (aka my other baby) and for my thirtieth birthday I gave my (well-paid, stable) communications advisor job the heave-ho for the heady world of self-employment. And here we are!

Bottom line, low key (as the cool kids say), I *freakin'* love writing. Love it. To the point where it's now my livelihood, my profession, my passion and my obsession. So why doesn't everyone love writing?

A NOTE ON SOURCES

The technicalities and frameworks of writing make me geek out like little else which makes me decidedly non-fun to talk with about books. I go straight to the construction and the craft, which apparently some people find boring. Humph. Anyhoo, for this reason, for over twenty years I've stashed craft techniques in my writing notebooks. I have tons of them, too many to count (quietly warbles the melody of *My Way*) and I'm far too superstitious to chuck them out, despite them taking up an entire shelf of my bookcase. Before you imagine an immaculately ordered, bullet journal-esque state of play, let me assure you, the reality is vastly different. The state of my notebooks isn't admirable in the slightest. Possibly aligned to the level of excitement I had when taking the notes, the original sources of writing strategies, ideas and techniques aren't always recorded. Some are like writing folklore that have been handed down through generations upon generations of writers. My notebooks between 2005-2007 are particularly messy—this is when I completed my Master of Arts (Writing and Literature) and gold in terms of approaches and technique are scattered across every page. Years ago, I was listening to a podcast where the guest took credit/ownership of an outlining technique that's been used since cavemen used rocks for plotting and I nearly drove my car off the road in outrage. This is my long-winded way of explaining that 'my' insights aren't necessarily conceived by me. Where I can locate sources I'll include them. At the back of this book is a non-exhaustive list of some of my favourite writing resources and references.

So on that note—let's do this!

Chapter Two

OBSTACLES AND ROADBLOCKS

MY MINI-RESEARCH PIECE

One lovely lockdown evening, I ran an online workshop for a professional organisation about connecting their story to their brand through beautiful content marketing. In the obligatory chat box, I asked people to share with me how they felt about the 'writing' part of their work, specifically writing about themselves and their brand. The responses came thick and fast, to the point where I had to stop reading as I was turning into a nodding bobblehead. I didn't want anyone to think their Wi-Fi was glitching. None of the responses particularly surprised me; there's little I haven't heard before after being in this game for decades, but what was particularly sobering and humbling was that some of the responses were coming from people that I knew had read my book *Tell Your Story*. Let me repeat that—

they'd already read my action-based guide for sharing their story, yet still struggled with the actual telling.

> *'I am inclined to think that what stands in the way of most personal writing is not technique but psychology: What's needed is the emotional preparedness and the generosity, if you will, to be honest and open to exposure.'*
>
> ~ Phillip Lopate

I'm inclined to agree! I believe that every brand—personal or professional—has a story to tell. Some people don't necessarily struggle with writing, per se. But writing about themselves? Hell no! Ask them to write about themselves and it's like asking them to run up a set of stairs Rocky style, wearing nothing but some strategically placed tassels. In fact, I've had people tell me they'd rather do anything, even play around with numbers in a spreadsheet (shudders) than sit down and write about themselves. The comments in that chat box cemented this theme. For almost twenty years, I've worked with people to tell their story, and while I have a solid insight and understanding into what completely exasperates people about writing, it's purely anecdotal. I've never really done a deep dive into the actualities. If 2020 taught us anything, it's sourdough is a massive PITA. It also taught us that now is as good a time as ever to take a good look under the hood of things.

Under the hood peeked I!

I wrote a spiffy little survey with the basic purpose of uncovering why people struggle with writing in general, and about themselves more specifically. I had a super-quick turnaround—one week from promotion to close-off—and I sweetened the deal with a 'lil Word Nerd giveaway to encourage completion. I put a call out for responses across LinkedIn with a better-than-I-possibly-could-have expected response—218 fabulous people took an average of 12 minutes out of their day to share their insights with me in as much or as little detail as they pleased.

The general 'vibe of the thing' for my survey was answering the question about what holds people back from telling their story. Is it their writing prowess? Is it their (*don't go there, don't do it*) mindset? (*You did it, didn't you?*) The people who responded were a mix of people with their own businesses and people who worked primarily in leadership roles in corporate and not-for-profit organisations. I wanted both those two groups so I had a nice balance of people who were writing for a business brand as well as a personal brand.

That said, my mini-research piece is exactly that—mini! It wasn't meant to be an extensive cross-section of the world of work. Initially, I didn't even have it in my lockdown-rattled mind that the insights I unearthed would be inspiration for a book! Instead, I was thinking that I could maybe come up with a cool workshop or program to fill knowledge gaps, but as I read the responses, I knew that "there's gold in 'dem thar hills!"

So, here's the questions I asked and the answers I received:

Where's home?

Want to hear something interesting? 94.5% of respondents were based in Melbourne. Hello, lockdown upon lockdown equals time to ponder and perhaps procrastinate!

What's your preferred communications channel for your brand? And why?

Things became really interesting here—69% of people preferred email communications, while the three main platforms (LinkedIn, Facebook and Instagram, in that order of preference) all lurked in the low 60% range. Next in line was communicating via speaking, workshops and events (50.8%), followed closely by networking (perish the thought) which came out at 43.1%, just a smidge ahead of blogging (41.5%) #ouchies. Finally, video came in at a sad little 27.7% as respondent's preferred communications channel. Written content for the win! That sense of connection and engagement via eyeballing someone in real time? Also clearly important.

This kicked me off down another thought spiral— what if people preferred workshops, speaking, events and networking because they didn't know how to leverage the power of writing to have the same, if not more impactful, brand-building possibilities? One of the comments against this question seemed to confirm this sneaking suspicion:

I have a preference to connect with people I know, who have common connections or a have a common interest/work purpose. That means some of my story or background may already be known.

I received so many responses to the why of this question, the themes of which I'll share as we proceed through these pages, but my favourite?

Why? Because you told me to ;-)

Next question: Which of the following best describes your approach to content marketing?
- I'm spontaneous, wild and free and so I share content according to what's going on in my life, personally and professionally (29.2%)
- Ugh, it's either radio silence or it's a flurry of activity (23.1%)
- I have a detailed content strategy, aligned to my broader goals that I roll out consistently (21.5%)
- I outsource as much as humanly possible (6.2%)

Which of the following is most important for you right now?
- Building your positioning and profile (60.9%)
- Increased leads and new clients (57.8%)
- Getting visible online (48.4%
- Finding your target audience and/or ideal client (43.8%)
- Improving your competitive advantage (20.3%)
- Shifting your positioning and profile (17.2%)
- Other (7.8%)

This question, from my perspective, was about aligning story to purpose, and more specifically, about aligning activities and resources against this purpose. It would tell me why people were dabbling in content marketing, beyond 'Because Holly said so,' although that's always a good answer. All of the answers are valid reasons to put consistent effort into writing. Content marketing is a slow burn, but as I've said to the point of kill-me-now it's also a highly powerful one, which does build profiles, and increases leads—and the *right* leads—as well as providing that edge commercially. However, what I didn't add as an option, and I bloody should have, is that writing provides *clarity*, both for the audience but also for the writer. In fact, one of my respondents who chose 'Other' said:

Being clear and consistent in my messaging and what I offer, and then building my audience and clients on this basis.

Boom!

Another said their priority was:

Getting some clarity. Am feeling a little lost with everything going on at the moment.

Double boom!

Let's have some fun: Imagine I had branding super-powers (I totally do, BTW) or was a genie and could make anything happen, what wish would you make my command? For your brand? For your business overall?

I left this question completely open-ended and the answers didn't disappoint. The responses had everything from fabulous clients in a gazillion dollar month, clarity over story and how to position it, standing out, validating creativity within a business offering, reaching the right people with the right message, to having the skills to get ideas out into the world and building the confidence to actually put written work in the public domain.

What's been your biggest professional challenge in the last twelve months?

Surprisingly, the c-word didn't rate much of a mention, given the vast, VAST majority of respondents did so during one of Melbourne's infamous five-day lockdowns that turned into how many months... gosh I don't even remember. They all blurred, didn't they? Anyhoo, the challenges that people shared really surprised me:

- Limiting beliefs
- Professional isolation
- Waning focus
- Losing momentum and a sense of relevance
- Marketing and standing out in a flooded marketplace
- Imposter syndrome and self-doubt
- Time management
- Consistency in showing up
- A loss of sponsors, aka having to tell their story rather than have their cheerleaders do it on their behalf
- Self-expression and being authentic rather than following tropes

What's your biggest struggle with your content?
- Finding the time for it—my plate is already so full with work, family and life (22.2%)
- Sounding different to my competitors and standing out (15.9%)
- Finding the mental space for writing—I don't have the headspace to craft my own content with my big to-do list (12.7%)

- The actual writing process of structuring my ideas and finding the words—words and I don't get along (11.1%)
- Finding the content that's relevant and useful (9.5%)
- What to write—I'm so overwhelmed by all the content that could/should be created. I don't know what to write (9.5%)
- I dislike my voice—when I can find it at all (3.2%)
- Procrastination and getting started (3.2%)
- Self-doubt (3.2%)
- Other: i.e. I hate talking about myself
- Consistency, knowing what to share and where, getting a return on what I put out. I hate talking about myself—what surprised me here was not a single person hit this little option button. At every workshop, every speaking gig, every networking event, at least one person says to me, 'I hate talking about myself.' This very comment sets off a chain reaction of nodding heads and screwed-up noses.

Some other comments that tickled my fancy:

Rambling on, not sounding too serious (I'm not like that in real life) not having enough of a mix of fun vs informative/educational.

The feeling of being stripped naked.

Care to elaborate on your struggles?

This was another open-ended question, the answers of which basically comprise the guts of this book. In fact, it was those answers that gave me the kick up 'le clacker' to turn what was initially a bit of a fun exercise to satisfy my curiosity into something much, much bigger, because it indicated a deeper need. Thus, this book.

What's your biggest fear for sharing your story?

I deliberated over including this question as although every single fear I listed had been disclosed to me multiple times, it felt like I was validating or giving airtime to fears that I wanted to dismantle. However, there's nothing like shining a light on the shadows to... well, whatever the metaphor is, the point being, let's obliterate those fears!

– Sounding boring (26.2%)
– Being judged (18%)
– Being misinterpreted (13.1%)
– Breaching my privacy or my personal boundaries (8.2%)
– Saying the wrong thing (6.6%)
– Sounding stupid (1.6%)
– Other (26.2%)

Again, the 'Other' responses had so, so much gold, and the following is a beautiful summation:

I don't want to come across as a dickhead.

I feel ya!

This answer had my peri-menopausal self raising my fist in solidarity:

Brain and body have to be aligned to the process. My brain is often spinning in overtime at 2 am with the greatest of ideas— but my body is too tired to get out of bed!

So true.

The bottom line, high-level summary:

Telling your story is one thing. Owning it is a whole other thing.

> 'We have trouble connecting with our own confident writing voice that is inside all of us, and even when we do connect and write well, we don't claim it… There seems to be a gap between the greatness we are capable of and the way we see ourselves and, therefore, see our work.'
>
> ~ Natalie Goldberg

My 'lil survey confirmed both the quote above as well as my gut-feel perception that it's not unusual for people to struggle with both writing for their brand and writing in general. Hell, even some of my clients, those for whom I had written *incredible* content plans, that provided the front end 'what to write' answers still felt a bit blocked in turning the pieces I'd detailed in their content plans into writing to share with the world to tell their story and grow their brand.

It came down to three roadblocks: mindset, technical skill or proficiency and the logistics of actually finding the time to write.

Overall, people were worried about being too salesy as they told their story. They felt stuck in ideation damnation—too many ideas, not enough ideas, or not knowing how to develop ideas. They didn't know how to sound different and felt like their writing priorities were unclear. They were concerned about being judged or misinterpreted, sounding boring or sounding stupid. Hashtag awkward!

What's the impact of *not* telling your story? From a communications perspective, it can have a significant impact on the success of any marketing efforts. This goes for personal brands as well as businesses, and it's just as applicable to people with product-based businesses as it is to service-based businesses. While a product should be front and centre, it doesn't change the fact that the 'About' page is still the most clicked page on any given website. Story is one of the most powerful tools all of us have at our disposal. Story is how we connect to people and encourage them to relate to us and resonate with our message, with the ultimate goal of influencing their behaviour in a way that benefits us, as mercenary as that may sound.

While I'd never want to dismiss the mindset roadblocks, the fear, anxiety about judgement, the feeling of being stripped naked, feeling irrelevant or self-indulgent, the sheer *ick* factor, my superpower is in the doing. I honestly believe that by sharpening up the toolkit, the mindset takes care of itself. Technical proficiency can crowd out these elements, and conversely lack thereof feeds them.

Thanks to the generosity of the people who completed my survey, I had a good idea of what holds people back from telling their story. And so, like a good Word Nerd, I got out a stack of index cards, scribbled down answers, ideas, thoughts and hypotheses and slowly began arranging them into themes and a structure of what would become this book.

What is it about mindset and writing? I was flicking through a book about drawing technique at my local library one afternoon, which is highly unusual for me. You see, I'm not visual, which is the grown up version of teenage Holly claiming, 'I'm not arty,' which stops me picking up a pencil for anything other than writing. Feel that shift in the force? That's my (wonderful!) clients who specialise in Emotional Intelligence yelling, 'Yet! I'm not visual *yet*!' as they read that line. I vaguely know where this horribly closed mindset came from—the students who were 'good' at art were hailed by one specific art teacher, whereas the rest of us were either ignored at best, or derided at worst. Back then, I was clearly given the message that I couldn't draw and I believed it. The book in question, *Drawing on the Right Side of the Brain* by Betty Edwards grabbed my attention with this statement:

> 'To many people, the process of drawing seems mysterious and somehow beyond human understanding.'

It's true! I have many friends who have no qualms in picking up a paintbrush or a sketching pad and just going for it, with magic pouring forth effortlessly. They're just talented, born with it, arty types. Or are they? Do I have a natural talent for writing? I've always been told I'm good at writing, aside from the aforementioned first year nursing assignment blip. I don't find writing off-putting or unpleasantly difficult. Writing is not something I wrestle with—if I do, it's a joyful wrestle, rather than an excruciating, mind-numbing, maths-like one. But this concept of natural talent doesn't do justice to my years of education and the time and effort spent honing my craft, including making writing central to my profession as well as my vocation. Let's not even mention the money I've spent over the years building my toolkit. At the same time I was pondering the link between natural talent and outcome, I stumbled upon a doco called '*I'm not a Runner*' about a group of people who emphatically denied they were runners, despite, in fact, running the New York Marathon. How on earth could people who ran a marathon not allow themselves the title of runner?

This led me to ask the question—why do so many people struggle with seeing themselves as 'good' at writing? Why did so many of the people who completed my survey believe their lack of writing skills held them back? I think I might have something of an answer, thanks to *Drawing on the Right Side of the Brain*:

> '*Many adults often related to me their painfully clear memories of someone ridiculing their attempts at drawing … Therefore, to protect the ego from further damage, they react defensively and understandably so: they seldom ever attempt to draw again.*'

I connect with this intimately—my negative art subject experience made me dislike art as a practice and not see it as remotely pleasurable, to the point that decades later I don't even enjoy colouring for leisure.

So, what even is a good writer? Writing isn't necessarily a talent bestowed upon the lucky few by capricious gods. While it certainly comes easier to some than others, it is a proficiency. But what makes a writer 'good?' At the bare bones, it's someone who knows how to make the very most out of the art and science that is writing, in order to illicit a response in a reader. From a business perspective, it's all about the entertain, educate, influence and inform factors adding up to the broader goal of making it rain money. Lord knows, social media-worthy office plants don't come cheap!

The concept of defining a good writer by default includes detailing what makes for a bad writer. That's a path I don't really want to go down, particularly given the very reason this book came into being was because I had incredibly accomplished people believing their writing abilities held them back from telling their story.

Instead, let's look at what writers (self-defined as good, bad or indifferent) do which makes them writers, that, when given focus and priority, builds their practice and their confidence in their abilities.

Good writers *read*. They read a lot. They're the ones who have a constant refrain to their nearest and dearest, honed over many, many years: 'Just lemme finish this page.' They are voracious. They read widely across genres and are known for spending far too long in bookshops. They're often the people who, regardless of what you say, can rattle off a book recommendation relevant to whatever the topic of conversation is.

They are curious observers to the point of intrusive. They notice details that other people don't. They're the ones you want on your table at a trivia night. Aka me. They're also the ones who tell you, 'I'll meet you at that cafe with the red seats,' despite the seats being changed many years ago. Also me. Ahem.

They take detailed notes. Very detailed. Also everywhere. They're people who love to research, the more thorough and accurate the better. They have random and not-so-random pieces of information in notebooks, in the notes app of their phone, emailed to themselves, in voice messages and some of them have enough sticky notes to paper an entire Scottish castle.

While they might not consider themselves storytellers, watch them in meetings of disparate groups. They can get to the point from different angles depending on the audience.

They're besotted with language! They collect words and turns of phrase and when they find new, interesting and unexpected ways to weave them together? They're in raptures. There may or may not be some hand-clapping and some high-pitched giggling. Again, OK, me.

They have a high respect for the rules and conventions of language and good writing, sometimes to their own detriment when they are so overwhelmed or intimidated that they can't banish the blank page. However, rules and conventions exist for a reason—this is how we both give expression to our beliefs, ideas, intellectual property and thoughts, but also how we share them in a way which allows others to connect. When it comes to writing for a brand, good writing becomes essential rather than a nicety. Brand writing is not the place for Joyce-esque prose, or absent grammar. Clear and concise over confusing and convoluted for the win. Every time.

So, how does this link to the concept of better writing? What does it mean to write better?

Chapter Three

COMMUNICATIONS ALIGNMENT AND PLANNING

NON-MERCENARY WRITING

Before I get stuck into the nitty-gritty of writing better as a way to get past that awful feeling of being 'stuck' I do have a little somethin' I'd like to get off my chest.

While I happily will write for the sake of writing, for the sheer joy it gives me, this is a different purpose to that of writing for my brand or my business. Business writing requires a strategic approach, one that's aligned to broader goals and messages. It also requires a solid handle on positioning. How do you want your brand perceived? This will determine the gap between a process (writing a blog post for example) and the finished product (hitting 'publish' on said blog post).

Here's my little cranky pants confession: I get more than a little shirty with an approach to business writing that's all about getting it done rather than getting it done well, especially if a brand has ideals, values and aspirations that are all about quality, trust, insight and depth.

Do you know the secret to good, compelling writing? Yes, it's clever syntax, clear messaging and audience alignment. Over the coming chapters I'll be sharing some of my favourite craft techniques to elevate your writing, from the bog-standard active vs passive voice, to the power of sensorial details. However, beyond craft, the secret weapon behind writing that grabs you by the ears is a writer who gives a flying you-know-what about the way they're crafting a message, i.e. the act of writing, as well as actually writing for a purpose that goes way beyond the end product.

> '*Focused on process, our creative life retains a sense of adventure. Focused on product, the same creative life can feel foolish or barren.*'
>
> ~ Julia Cameron

I'd like to add one more adjective to foolish or barren, and that's mercenary. Let me explain.

People write for a number of reasons. They write to showcase their hard-earned expertise and experience, to share their story in a way that makes a difference, to influence their positioning as a go-to in their space and for sheer, unadulterated, fork-yeah bragging rights.

None of these reasons are any less valid than the others—who, for example, doesn't love a good FIGJAM session? What I do take to task, however, is writing without giving a shit, and writing without giving due attention to the full process.

Fancy a story?

An author delivered a guest lecture for my Creative Non-Fiction class during my Master of Writing and Literature. Their process for writing a book was to choose a social issue (i.e. corruption, financial shenanigans, demonising people with mental illness) and write against that. Their reasoning— it would sell. Full stop. And their writing showed that. Clearly. Unequivocally. When you don't care about your content, it shows. When you bang it out quickly and don't care enough to bother going back to edit and rework it, *it shows.*

The thing about writing, and writing well, is that except for those rare AF moments when the angels sing and the glitter flies, it's really hard. Really, *really* hard at times. There's an adage amongst writers; 'I hate writing but I love having written,' and this has been regurgitated in different ways by writers as diverse as George RR Martin (Mr. Game of Thrones) to Dorothy Parker. I love how it conveys that battle between the euphoria of creating and accomplishment and the gut-churning stress of facing the empty page.

So, what is writing well, and the process? Writing well only happens when writing (funny that), and people can only fully step into the motivations I shared above when their writing embraces the full life cycle of writing. I've had someone tell me that they hate their self-published book, to the point of not promoting it at all in their communications plan. It's not even included on their LinkedIn profile. They cringe when they think of it, believing they rushed its publication after the completion of the first draft. With only a brief copyedit from a kind mate, they believe that it's not even close to a reflection of their best work. This is devastating!

Good work takes time and space. It takes immersion in the process as well as in the actual subject matter itself. It doesn't happen with writing that's dashed off quickly, that merely scrapes the surface. Good writing needs considered thought, as well as depth of thought. It involves scribbles, staring out the window, more scribbles when lightbulbs go off, testing and teasing of ideas, and manhandling and manipulating information. I'm talking quality over quantity. I'm talking showing up fully.

That's not to say a first draft can't be knocked out quickly—of course it can, but what I find frustrating is when people blithely disregard the fact that the first draft is just the beginning. I would argue that the first draft is simply the launchpad for the *real* writing. It's the starting point. The revision and rewrite is where the magic happens and a first draft, an average collection of words, sentences and paragraphs, becomes good writing. In fact, each year, on 1 December, after 30 days of writing insanity, NaNoWriMo* (more below) starts their 'Now What' campaign. Their number one piece of advice after finishing a first draft? Under no circumstances send it to an editor or publisher. Why? Because if you've done it right, it should be a huge, steaming pile of crap.

> 'Only God gets it right the first time and only a slob says, "Oh well, let it go, that's what copyeditors are for."'
>
> ~ Stephen King

After the crap comes the good stuff—writers get to pull things apart, kill their darlings, mess things up, stick their conclusion at the beginning, or if necessary, where the sun doesn't shine. It's where you might challenge the assumptions you wrote as your first draft—often your beliefs shift and evolve as you explore them via writing. This is clarity. This is critical thinking brought to life.

It's extending, questioning and finessing. It's leaning in hard on the techniques that writers use to amplify the impact of their words. It's a chance to craft something you're really, truly proud of, an accurate and powerful representation of you, and your smarts. This can't happen in a hurry. It simply can't.

This isn't an argument against productivity—of course, it's important to be productive, efficient and effective in our writing habits. But just as important as getting it done (which is the whole premise behind my batch writing program and events) is to go deep rather than shallow, to prioritise robust consideration rather than quick thinking. This means creating an outline to stop you going rogue with your content or from missing an integral piece of information, and it means including thinking, *deep thinking,* before, during and after the first draft. We've all experienced that delicious explosion of ideas, long after our fingers have left the pen or keyboard. This is your subconscious bubbling away. When you write in a hurry, for the sheer sake of getting something done, then you're focused on the end product rather than the process, which will be to the detriment of your work.

Yes, you can write anything in fifteen minutes, an hour, a day, a weekend, a week, a month—but know clearly, intimately, and irrevocably, that what you've written is a first draft. Focusing on the product rather than the process risks settling for whatever comes out in the first sitting, and guess what? It isn't going to be your best work. Not even close. Is it hard, approaching writing as a process? Oh hell yes, it can be, to the point of screaming. But is it worth it? Double hell yes. It means you're fully showing up and you're going for quality, not just ticking something off your list. And spoiler alert—if you work with me, you don't get a choice. We're going for deep, not trite, but I'm by your (writing) side the whole way.

So, my goal for this book is to get you unstuck and to make writing a less onerous, handwringing or stultifying process. It's also to have you writing well and sharing writing that's reflective of the incredible work you do. No wham, bam, thank you ma'am, on my watch! OK, perhaps that metaphor doesn't really fit, but it's something I've been wanting to weave into a business book for many a year.

* National Novel Writing Month, aka NaNoWriMo is a not-for-profit organisation I stumbled upon at university which I thought sounded like a sure-fire path to rocking inconsolably in a corner. I was right, but also wrong. The concept of NaNoWriMo is to write every day in November, around 1,600 words a day, with the support of a global community of writers doing the same thing. It started out as a fiction writing challenge and has the aim of unfettered writing, writing without editing or second-guessing yourself. The goal is a completed first draft that is to be strictly viewed as such.

READER BEFORE WRITER

Brand and business writing is all about intent and purpose. At the very crux of this is the end recipient, the actual human who will be reading your work. Who are you talking to? Having this person in mind from the get-go makes picking up that pen (how very quaint) or attacking the keyboard so much easier. What's the story I should focus on for this person?

So, who is this elusive reader of yours? Let's make them less elusive. What is this person wanting to achieve? What are this person's pain points and problem areas? How do they feel about their current situation? Here's a quick hint: they'll tell you this in their very first contact with you, where they say 'Hey, I see you do x, and I need help with y.' Dig a little deeper and ask them why they feel they need help. What language do they use to describe their pain points, their fears and frustrations? Get specific—what are the words and phrases they use? This is the answer to 'What's the impact of us not working together, of you not changing how you address something in your current situation?' What have they done in the past to try and resolve this? Why did it/has it miserably failed? What are your services/products that can help this person achieve their desires?

Let's bring this to life in the context of this book that you're holding in your hot 'lil hands, as I wrote it to answer those questions listed above.

This book is for people who feel stuck with their writing. They know that the written word is an incredibly powerful way to make a connection with others in the context of their work, yet every time they sit down to write they either can't come up with any ideas, have too many ideas, or when they write it's like the incarnation of their best Year Nine English essay lies squirming on the page. Their writing feels boring, overwhelming, confusing, scattered or an ungodly blend of all of the above.

When I'm thinking about audiences, it's not often I go down the avatar path. You can, and many of my colleagues in the communications or marketing space believe you should. While I'm a sucker for detail, honestly? I'm OK with a bare bones approach to locking down what you know about your audience. Namely, who are they? Who is your typical client? This is the sort of information that often gets buried within the pages of a business plan, but it's the type of content that can be really powerful when it comes to brands, because it basically defines the question—am I your people? The more deeply you understand your dream client, the more you will have in terms of content to communicate how your solutions can resolve their issues. Your messages will write themselves.

Here's another example that I tend to trot out a lot because it's just so damn clear: imagine you are a personal trainer specialising in fat loss for women over 40 who are time poor. The messages to target this audience will be completely different to those of a personal trainer who works with male clients in their twenties who want to enter body building competitions.

Let's bring this to life—shall we have some fun scribbling? Grab some scrap paper and a timer.

Think about who you'd love to work with, if they were your sole client until the end of time, the one client you could spend all your time working with, who would they be? Sometimes, it's easy to do this by taking a quick scan of your existing and former client list and making note of the clients and the work that lit you up, that felt like such a guilty pleasure that you almost felt bad taking their money. Almost... While you're here, think about what led them to you—what were their triggers for picking up the phone or sending you an email to explore working with you? Now, let's dig a little deeper and go beyond the practicalities of what you do. For example, your Numbers Nerd might do your bookkeeping and lodge your BAS statement, but they also free up time and space. Let's not forget that they remove stress and uncertainty.

Set your timer for 10 minutes and scribble against those thoughts. Try to write in full sentences rather than dot points and don't overthink it. You're scribbling on scrap paper, not carving out the Ten Commandments.

When your timer goes off, you'll have a beautiful collection of scribbles that will give clarity about who you are speaking to with your communications, as well as why they should give a flying you-know-what about what you have to say. This means that when it comes to writing for a communications tactic (social media post, blog post, email campaign, even your elevator pitch for a specific event) you are in a better situation to craft a message that aligns to both your goals and to the motivations of your audience. When a message speaks to the right person—boom! Connection! Here's an idea: why don't you turn all those scribbles into an overarching blog post that tells the story of who you work with?

SPECIAL, JUST LIKE A SNOWFLAKE

If audience is the 'who' in communications, then what is the 'what?' Enter the Unique Value Proposition. If I had a dollar for every time a client asked me for help to succinctly describe their work without sounding boring, I'd have at least $3,224 by now. At least! Sometimes we are far too close to our work to see the detail, or maybe it's the other way around—while we're deep in the trenches we can't see the bigger picture. This is where a spot of staring out the window comes into play.

What's a left of centre way you've solved a problem lately? What is your special approach to doing things that your competitors/colleagues don't? What are the common misconceptions about you, your work or your industry? What do new clients need/want to know about your business and your work? What is it that time and time again you get asked about in terms of your work or your industry? What is it you wished you were asked about your work? We're looking for the who, what, how and why in your work and we're going to nail it in one or two sentences. In business planning and marketing circles they call this your Unique Value Proposition or UVP, and this is where the gold is.

There are plenty of UVP templates out there but a lovely simple one I tend to favour is:

I work with {insert client description} to {insert client's goal} by {insert your service}.

Want a couple of examples?

Imagine you're a professional organiser differentiating yourself within a thriving, competitive industry market:

I help busy working mothers free up their mental load by creating sustainable, effective systems and routines to get more out of their day.

Or

You're a dietitian who specialises in prepubescent and adolescent nutritional health:

I help schools meet their healthy eating obligations by guiding their messaging to parents as well as their onsite food providers.

One more, just for the fun of it!

You're a business coach working within a specific high-performance model and approach:

I help executives and leaders in the corporate space to elevate their performance without burning out.

What's yours? Pop on the timer and get scribbling!

SUPERCHARGED COMMUNICATIONS

Here's a quick one for you—have a think about every piece of communications collateral that crosses your path each day, from emails and social media, right through to customer experience. Some will have an indisputable impact on you, others will barely register. Want to know the difference between the two? One is supercharged through strategy, the other is scattergun.

'Humans are wired for story. We hunt for and respond to certain specific things, regardless of the genre. Why is this so? Because story is the language of the brain. We think in story.'

~ Lisa Cron

Communications storytelling is simply taking advantage of this language and is the means by which people become aware of your brand in the context of creating a desired response. Put even more simply—you have a goal, you have an audience, communications is what brings the two together. You might say it's the bridge, if, like me, you love a good metaphor in the morning. The more thought and strategy that goes into communications, the more effective it will be and the less likely the bridge is going to end in a *Speed*-like drop off into nothing. OK, enough with the bridge metaphor!

Communications broadly, and content marketing specifically, is the articulation of your promise to your audience. When we identify a product or a service that will make our clients' lives just that little bit sweeter, the question becomes; how can we communicate that simply, clearly and effectively? How do we make sure the story we're sharing with them is set up for success? This is where taking the time to align your audience and message to communications in the context of the broader goal really comes into play. Of course, I have the perfect acronym for the process, one which has driven more than a handful of clients to distraction due to how hard it is to say without undue spitting:

G.A.M.T.E.R.

Goal—Audience—Message—Tactic—Evaluate—Refine.

Ah, poetry in motion, am I right? Let's move our way through it:

Goal: what is the goal for this specific *thing* in your business? e.g. sell out a new program.

Audience: who is the most appropriate person it's directed towards? e.g. women who see themselves as people-pleasers.

Message: how can we share in the clearest possible way what we want people to know? e.g. my new program shares practical strategies to remove that awful jolt of resentment we experience when our people-pleasing tendencies stop us living our best life.

Tool: what is the best way to deliver that message, to this audience, to meet this goal? e.g. webinar, speaking at target audience events.

Evaluate: how'd we go? Did our audience connect with our message to the point where we sold out our program?

Refine: What should we do next time? Was the webinar a big fat flop? Did the mention in the weekly newsletter trigger a flurry of sign-ups?

Spending a quick fifteen minutes getting down and GAMTER-ing (look at me, always trying to make 'fetch' happen) before you write is a powerful way to give your communications a head start. This is connecting story to purpose in action with a focus on the why, the what and the so-now-what. It's a clear framework that gives clarity of audience and of message. As I've said for a long, long time, to the point where I even had it printed on postcards, clarity looks gorgeous on you.

BRINGING A VISION TO LIFE

So we know who we want to speak with and what we want them to know via our writing—what's the best way to make the two tango? Now we step into the territory of vision. Stick with me; we'll get through this together.

In *Tell Your Story* I shared a story about vision—every art class story starts with an anecdote of a journalist visiting an artist and asking how they're going to turn a chunk of marble into a sculpture of a philosopher staring (philosophically, of course) off into space. The artist's cheerful answer? 'Easy peasy, lemon squeezy. I just take away the parts that don't look like a philosopher.' This is vision and it informs everything.

Vision is having a vague idea of not only what you're going to write, but why you're writing it. I'm not talking about your why here in terms of showcasing your expertise, or making a difference, of influencing or positioning yourself in the broader context of your business or brand, but rather the 'why' in the context of this writing from the perspective of your reader. What's in it for them? So what? What's the point? Why is this important to your end reader, your audience? What do you want to achieve from sharing this message? You could also think about this in terms of purpose, or your argument or conviction for something, or your solution to a problem.

The vision becomes reality when what you want a reader to actually know is aligned to a structure to enable or facilitate that. Every story could be structured with facts, opinions, descriptions, observations, memes, quotes, references, citations, anecdotes or questions. The fun, and the writing, comes into play when we pair the right structural components with the vision for the piece. I'm talking interviews, Q&As, personal stories, behind the scenes, case studies, how-to guides, editorials, listicles (and yes, that made me smirk too), thought pieces, reviews and frequently asked questions.

So, in the words of *that* campaign: what the bloody hell are we writing here? That is the question. I'm never one to shy away from a Shakespeare reference.

The most simple example is actually really big, and that's the process of turning ideas into a book. A book's structure is more powerful and effective when aligned to its purpose. Is it instructional or educational? Is it evocative of the process of working with you? Is it sharing life lessons with an intent to inspire a change in behaviour? All of these questions will determine if it should be linear (i.e. chronological or logically step-based, like a recipe) or non-linear or even circular, where the book starts and ends at the same place. Of course, there are also old-school structures like the three act storytelling technique that you've seen in a gazillion movies: beginning, middle with conflict to be overcome, and end. I love three act structures because they can be linear, non-linear or even circular with some wrangling. They're logical, and most importantly of all they provide clarity for both the writer and the reader. Best of all, it can be used in something as huge as a book all the way down to a long-form social media caption.

In terms of writing within three acts, it's about creating a flow of information that makes sense. Put yourself in your reader's position and think about how logical the flow of information feels. Think also about the order of importance. How is this going to be most impactful? Can some of the individual points be combined? If you have one idea that's chock-a-block with complexity, should you split that up into different pieces of copy?

When it comes to readability, it's good practice that each point made in a piece of writing must 'cause' or inspire the next. We're not going for the random 'this one time, at band camp' vibe here. We want each point to build upon the one before in some way. We want it to be clear why each point matters. It's also a good idea to keep in mind some (logical) inclusions of stories of conflict, suspense, levity or interest may keep it flowing and make it more engaging for the reader. When I ask, 'What are we writing?' I'm going back to what I always bang on about. Purpose and intent. Let that inform the structure.

> 'Communication is about telling a story with a purpose, and by using the writerly tools of shape, plot and address, the aim is to persuade the audience that the story is true or has value (conviction).'
>
> ~ Craig Batty and Sandra Cain

My view is that the purpose will inform the writerly tools. While I'm a sucker for a long, immersive read, sometimes I just want the short and sharp. When we're time poor and overwhelmed, we just want to be told to do something simple; we don't want to wade through three paragraphs of chatter before we get to the good, practical stuff that's going to change our life. When I was a nurse, back when dinosaurs roamed the earth, I'll never forget a professor of gerontology claiming that sometimes, one of the best ways to support/treat someone presenting with confusion is to give them a drink of water. You see, dehydration can cause confusion, and what could be seen as 'dementia' might in fact just be someone who hasn't had a drink for far too long. Think about the expertise you hold. Is there a way you can simply tell someone to drink more water? These quick wins are content that serves a need. They also build trust.

I'll be sharing more about structures in the Writer's Toolkit section. Bring it!

Chapter Four

BRAINSTORMING LIKE A BOSS

IDEAS, IDEAS EVERYWHERE!

Confession time—I don't believe in writer's block. That's not to say that I never struggle for content ideas, but I see that as more of a depletion of mojo. I know that for many people, coming up with the stuff to write about in their business is one of the things that keeps them up at night. Some people lose half a day struggling to squeeze out some words for their email list. Some people try and write every page of their website for far too long. Sometimes people feel like they're writing the same thing over and over and over again for social media, and other people feel just completely over it because they find that constantly coming up with ideas is exhausting.

There's an emotional, financial, and personal impact from feeling blocked. But most importantly, writer's block robs people of the chance to get to know you and then buy from you or work with you. We know that people buy from people they like, and people get to know you through the stories you tell. And the stories that you tell are should be a way to feel energised by what you do, not drained. I know you're busy, juggling a million things. You know you need to post, but you don't need one more decision or to waste time over-analysing every possibility, or staring out the window fretting about what to write.

I work with two kinds of clients—those who have so many ideas to write about that they're absolutely drowning in them. The other type draw a complete blank when it's time to write for their brand.

While this book is about writing better, we can't do that until we have something to actually write about. Now's the time to collect, curate and catalogue ideas for your dream content marketing plan.

I'm talking anything and everything that could possibly be included. As they say in the classics, no idea is stupid, which we all know isn't true. We're going to capture them anyway, because when you're mining ideas, there is incredible gold to be discovered in the rubble of stupid.

Hello, brainstorming, you crafty minx, you! Brainstorming is fun, energising, no holds barred. The goal is to collect a bucketload of writing ideas for your brand. With a bucketload of ideas, it's almost impossible not to feel inspired and enthusiastic as you share your story in a way that feels right.

This chapter is all about coming up with ideas for your brand. Of course, the editing and curating, voice and point of view are a whole different kettle of fish. Don't worry, that fish can be fried later. But first, you need that pool of ideas to play with.

There's lots of different approaches to brainstorming. At one end of the scale, think of an idea or a topic relating to your brand or your work, then brain dump like there's no tomorrow. Think of all the bits and bobs that you could include against that topic.

Here's an example:

Imagine a personal stylist thinking about style in the era of online meetings. What could be included against this topic? It might be accessories. It might be cuts and colours for the zoom screen or positioning on camera. It might be some stats and research about the impact of what you wear on how you feel. It might even answer that age-old question—should I wear pants today?

Another approach is to start with a big picture and a plan for the time period ahead, such as a week, month or a year. When it comes to something more established, like a blog plan, I like to have a year's worth of content plotted out in advance. Some people like to go with monthly themes, and they link that to holidays, seasonal activities, things that are happening in their professional life and personal life. Some like to brainstorm against the core topics for their brand or their industry. Themes lend themselves beautifully to a brainstorming session.

Get yourself some more scrap paper and your timer. Set it for ten minutes and then scribble down some ideas for your brand against these themes:

- Quick wins
- Momentum
- Clarity

- Consistency
- Authority
- Accessibility
- Grinds my gears
- Popular misconception

I'd bet my bottom dollar you could have five ideas against each, minimum, am I right?

I create content plans for clients using a pillar-based approach. The pillars we create for their brand's content marketing are tightly aligned to their broader business goals and positioning. It's content that ensures that whatever they're sending out is actually focused on how they want to be known. It's easier to write strategically, and it stops them being pigeonholed as something unwanted. The pillars I create for my clients start life as a structured, strategic, ridiculously fun brainstorming Q&A session, just like the pillars I've created for my own brand. One of my content pillars is communications. A brainstorm against that pillar automatically leads to ideas such as how to plan, how to decide which tactic is right for which message, the nuts and bolts of how to write for your brand, how to craft a story-based 'About' page. That's the basics—the how, the what. I also always love a why concept and the broader messaging and meaning behind the action-based content.

Another way to get ideas for your content is through thinking about the work that you actually do, work that you've completed. Think of a specific project, the principles behind it, how you did it, how you implemented it, and the outcome. Don't cringe, but this is a case study, or in more evocative language (and infinitely more fun for the word nerds amongst us) The Hero's Journey, and you can bet your cotton socks I'll be sharing more about that in the Writer's Toolkit section of this book.

I'm a sucker for a mind map as a brainstorming tool. Put a central word in the middle of a piece of paper, and then let your ideas prompted by that word flow. You can use mind maps for things like your service offerings, by imagining what they conjure up in the minds of your clients and the minds of your audience. Use them to spark words to create ideas for topics which in turn become your content.

Sometimes people's brains are so full of stuff that they feel devoid of creative, fresh ideas and inspiration. When you're feeling really stuck—and it happens to the best of us—dig into some writing prompts and watch the magic unfold. They're purposely designed to fire up inspiration and ignite imagination. They're not a new concept; I've been using writing prompts for forever, often in creative writing. I use them in my own business and with my clients almost every day. They're how I get words out of my head or client's heads and onto the page or screen. They're launch pads and they trigger us in all the good ways. I have a ton of videos on my Facebook page that share my favourite prompts. They include things like thinking about why people love working with you beyond the tangible benefits that you provide (hint—your testimonials, feedback and evaluation forms will help you out enormously here). Think about things like what makes you feel good about what you do? What is it that you dislike about your work, industry, profession, but you know is necessary? What stories in your work have you heard that make you laugh or shake your head in bewilderment? How do you react to the jibes and misconceptions people have about your work? What's the best feedback you've ever had? How is the real world experience of your work different from what you expected before you went into the job?

When you're doing a brainstorming session, the goal is to capture as many ideas as you possibly can. You want to fill that bucket with a wide range of ideas. Some might be more suitable for colloquial writing, such as your social media captions, while others might be for your blog posts. Some you might be able to structure into the outline of a book. As you go, you can also break up how you could potentially structure your ideas to keep it interesting for you and your audience. I'm talking instructions, tips and tricks, tutorials, checklists or hacks to overcoming a problem. You can do interviews with relevant people. You can do case studies. You can do reviews. There's almost always a place for a rant, good news stories, predictions and reviews.

Some ideas you won't be able to use. With brainstorming, unfettered, throw-caution-to-the-wind brainstorming, comes crap. There's no delicate way to say that; we all know that there are some shocking ideas! Some don't reveal their true state until they're laid out beside other ideas who deserve a seat at your content table. Others seem like they fit until the act of teasing an idea out via writing shows that while they might be good at first glance, they simply don't belong with your brand or against the specifics of what your goal is for something.

'Kill your darlings, kill your darlings, kill your darlings.'
~ Stephen King

So, when it comes to your ideas, what to kill? Does it add value or interest to your brand? In fiction or creative writing, we look at every side character and are ruthless about the role they play, the function they serve. This is in the context of moving a plot along, but this concept of making everything serve a purpose is equally as applicable to brand writing as it is for other forms. I have a folder full of fabulous ideas for which I can't find a brand fit but I can't seem to let go. Just like those tax receipts we keep for seven years—or whatever it is that your numbers nerd dictates—I do an almighty cull periodically and wonder what in the living hell I was thinking, or I give them a rework and fall in love with them again, or sometimes I gift them to a client who's a perfect fit.

Brainstorming and research, research and writing. Some people frown against mixing the act of brainstorming with research but to me they just play so nicely together. One of my favourite ways to research is reading literature reviews and following the breadcrumbs left by super-clever minds. This wide reading produces a ton of ideas for me and is an essential part of my process, but I also understand the refrains against it. Some people research and research and research, yet never move on to their own ideas or to the writing part of the process. The other reason I love a good research/ brainstorming session is because once on the other side of brainstorming, gaps are revealed. We love a gaping gap, a yawning chasm, don't we? This is where we consider if we've gathered everything we need by way of research. What *don't* I know? Do I need anything verified? Am I being a smidge half-arsed by attributing a quote I love to 'source unknown?' And yes, I am. Are some of my ideas assumptions I need to challenge? Is Imposter Syndrome really a thing or is it just the patriarchy? Spoiler alert: it's the patriarchy. Back to my point, and yes, I do have one. As you start brainstorming, you unearth what you don't know. As you research, you uncover more information than you could/should include in your content strategy. Some people research on the fly or as they go, other people like to research at the front end and use that to guide their progression. I'm a mix of both. You do you!

LIFE MAPPING, JOURNEY TIMELINING AND STORY BANKS

We've all had a lifetime of experiences and these are the potential cure to all our personal brand writing woes. The problem isn't just how to translate our own experiences (or those we've observed) into content that's appropriate and aligned, but how to actually nail them down, ripe for the retelling.

Life mapping or experience timelining is a super-fun way to spend some time and is perfect both for a spot of reflection as well as filling up your well of relatable and likeable content.

Basically, we're looking for key life moments that define who you are and how you came to be this shimmering version of yourself. 'Plot twist,' as the kids say. There are a couple of ways to do this. Some approaches call for a thematic process such as family, career/work, health, school and relationships. Others go for chronological, if not year by year, by season or decades such as early years, primary school, high school and entering the workforce. While I can't imagine you'd ever really write something that started with; 'I was born on a dark and stormy night,' in my mind it's much easier to set up a way of capturing memories and moments that's chronological.

There are many ways to attempt this. Some people love a spreadsheet with relevant columns and rows *breaks out in cold sweat*. Some love ye olde notebook with a year to a page. Creative, visual types love a giant sheet of paper and a fancy set of Pantone markers. Hell, you can bring out the sticky notes if so inclined. The main consideration is that this isn't often a one and done exercise. You'll find that once you choose how you're going to create your timeline or map and slap on the thinking cap, the ideas and memories will flow unbidden for quite some time.

So, what are you looking for? I'm a sucker for a significant transition, those 'Yer a wizard, Harry,' moments where, for better or worse, things flipped. Times of change, big and little, or a little incident that turned out to be not-so-little, and vice versa. Start with your major life events and what was happening beyond your immediate sphere of experience.

Other milestones and life events could be related to your education (starting school, leaving school, winning awards, being overlooked for awards), your career (first job, worst job), your relationships (the one that got away, enemies to friends, friends to enemies—why not lean into every Young Adult fiction trope here and have fun), travel, first experience of grief, your first taste of proper Italian pizza.

As you're collating and curating memories to list in your timeline or map, go for brevity. Under each marker, chronological or otherwise, make a quick note. This isn't about writing per se; it's about capturing an essence to give you a kickstart for the writing process later.

For example:

Memory: 26 January 2007—gave birth to first daughter
Content evolution of memory: On one stinkin' hot, late
January evening, when the vast majority of Australians were
downing beers and devouring over-barbecued sausages, my
older cherub was born.

How I arrived at this content evolution was via a memory
kickstart. Are you coming up blank? Take a look at what the
mind remembers, including your five senses. Did a certain
sound or smell really imprint itself in your memory? Which
seems most important? How do you express your emotional
experience of an event? Look for the strings of association
in your mind to help unlock ideas. Make notes, capture
the details, allow your mind to follow along the path the
memories laid. Where were you? What were you doing? How
were you feeling? How are you feeling now whilst recalling
this? Pick some random moments from your past, such as
your first day of school, a concert, a family get-together.
When you've chosen five or six, write about what you
remember about the experience. You don't have to search for
the particular memories or precise details, just write whatever
comes to mind. Do this for 10 minutes and then read back on
what you've written. Did you incorporate memorable sights,
smells, tastes, sounds? The little touches that mean so much
to you will create a tangible atmosphere in your work, one
that might feel like a real memory to everybody that reads it
as well as to you.

Want an incredible rumination on the link between
memory and writing? Have a read of 'Run fast, stand still,

or, the thing at the top of the stairs, or new ghosts from old minds,' an essay on creativity in *Zen in the Art of Writing* by Ray Bradbury. I went to a writing for children workshop where the presenter shared an exercise based on Bradbury's musings: I remember when...

Without thinking too much, write five sentences starting with 'I remember when...' against your life map. This is all about fun here, you may never ever publish 'I remember when my brother choked on a bee and crashed his BMX.' And herein lies my fist-bump/boom moment: don't think that every story has to be about huge, life shattering incidents that spun the earth on the axis. The everyday moments, the 'little' stories are where the colour and depth comes into play. These reflect status, passions, patterns and moments in time. Don't discount their power to convey a message!

Chapter Five

WRITER'S TOOLKIT

WHAT STOPS PEOPLE READING?

What stops people reading? Well, firstly, it's writing that's bogged down in too much detail or irrelevant information. Think about the most boring wedding speeches you've had the misfortune of sitting through. The speaker drones on and on while you try with increasing desperation to find a discreet way to hit the bar.

> *'All of us have stopped in the middle of a memo, an article, or a book realizing that while we may have understood its words and sentences, we don't quite know what they should all add up to.'*
>
> ~ Joseph M. Williams

This manifests in what I like to call the 'Sorry, what?' syndrome. From a brand perspective, it's someone waffling on about how they 'bring to life the digital arena of a brand' rather than telling you they're a web developer or designer. Here's a quick story to illustrate what I'm talking about:

In my mid-forties I reread *Beloved* by Toni Morrison. I had a copy of *Beloved* for years and tried and tried and *bloody tried* to read it, but just couldn't. The prose was just too ephemeral and I had to work too hard. I think my copy ended up at the school fair book stall eventually. After hearing that *Beloved* was one of Toni Morrison's later pieces, written post-midlife, where women creatives seem to step into a whole new sphere of 'stuffwhatyouthinkI'lldowhatIwant.' It's not a technical term, but I kinda like it. She threw all her magical skills at this story, took glorious risks and wrote her heart out. Reading *Beloved* perhaps a decade after putting it aside for the last time, I persevered. Somehow it wasn't as off-putting to me as I dove into the prose. But that's fiction, not writing for a brand. The second I read anything brand or business-related that makes me reread or second-guess it, I'm outta there. You want to influence me, to compel me, to entice me? Don't make me work for it!

In writing for a brand, clarity must, must, MUST come first. While you can be clever, there's no room for convoluted or confusing. Depending on your brand, cutesy might be off-limits too. We want people to keep reading! If they're bored, confused or offended they won't.

The other thing that's a killer to good writing is what Don Watson refers to as weasel words:

> '*It is cliche-ridden and lacks meaning, energy, imagery and rhythm. It also lacks words. It struggles to express the human. Buzz words abound in it. Platitudes iron it flat.*'
>
> ~ Don Watson

In my writing workshops, I sometimes share examples of such writing, and they're often courtesy of local government agencies who make it their mission to make their writing as impenetrable as possible. Here's a pearler with names and dollar amounts changed to keep my legal superstar happy:

Council supports Country Lanes of Australia seeking funding of $26 million for the implementation of the AnyTown Road transport infrastructure improvements in AnyTown township at Any Street intersection to tackle significant safety and access issues onto AnyTown Road. Current access and congestion issues are anticipated to worsen.

What the actual AnyTown are you saying here? What do I need to know as a resident?

Don Watson agrees:

'… all kinds of institutions cannot pass on the simplest information about their services without also telling us that they are *contemporary*, *innovative* and *forward-looking* and *committed to continuous improvement*, as if the decision to raise their rates or change their phone number can only be grasped in this *context-sensitive* way.'

One of my favourite episodes of *Utopia* is episode 7 in season 3 where Rob Sitch's character is handed a document from the Department of Defence to turn into a set of pithy messages. By 'favourite' I mean hive-inducing. I have very vivid memories of facing the same challenge. It's 200 pages of indecipherable, babbling gobbledegook with words like 'interoperability' which on reflection I'm not actually sure is a word.[1] It's baffling, and when it comes to writing for a brand, baffling is the last thing we want!

Jargonistic and dense language aside, some other issues I see in business and branding writing are introductions to blog posts or to sales pages that don't make sense or are too abstract against the information that follows, annoying repetition, sentences that are far too long or too short and blunt, passive writing (more on that soon!) and gaps in the information. Non-conventional formats and structures are another blocker. Poor grammar, particularly when a brand is heralding its attention to detail, is a hard pass.

THE G WORD...

'Grammar is not just a pain in the ass; it's the pole you grab to get your thoughts up on their feet and walking.'
~ Stephen King

King was loath to include too much about grammar in his ode to writing. Me too. There are plenty of resources, tools and books out there to show you where to stick an apostrophe and how to organise a sentence to make sense and make an impact. That said, my survey suggested that people get caught

---

1   It is, but it's pure weasel. ~ Holly's fabulous editor.

up in the nuts and bolts of writing and so I think it's important to have a brush up. To this end, permit me present to you a Victorian Schoolmistress' 10 Golden Rules of Punctuation.

A VICTORIAN SCHOOLMISTRESS' 10 GOLDEN RULES OF PUNCTUATION

- Sentences begin with a capital letter, so as to make your writing better.
- Use a full stop to mark the end. It closes every sentence penned.
- The comma is for short pauses and breaks, and also for lists the writer makes.
- Dashes—like these—are for thoughts by the way. They are called em dashes, because they're the size of a letter 'm'—pretty cool, hey? They insert extra information (and you can also use brackets for such observations).
- These two dots are colons: they pause and compare. They also do this: list, explain, and prepare.
- The semicolon makes a break; followed by a clause. It does the job of words that link; it's also a short pause.
- An apostrophe shows the owner of anyone's things, and it's also useful for shortenings.
- I'm so glad! He's so mad! We're having such a lark! To show strong feelings use an exclamation mark!
- A question mark follows What? When? Where? Why? and How? Do you? Can I? Shall we? Give us your answer now!
- 'Quotation marks' enclose what is said, which is why they're sometimes called 'speech marks' instead.

I've googled the living shizzle out of these 10 Golden Rules almost since before the times of Google. It grinds my convention-abiding gears that I've never been able to find a credible source. I have memories of chanting, 'I'm so glad! He's so mad!' in what must have been early primary school. Many decades later when I was in a lecture hall while completing MA Writing and Literature, my editing lecturer flashed it up on a projector. She actually had it on one of those transparencies which preceded laptops and interactive whiteboards and what-not. She'd dragged it around since the late '60s and was also unable to give it attribution. It's such a clean, clear way to keep the rules of grammar clear, so I share it here and await a middle of the night visit from the ghost of a Victorian School Mistress for not crediting her. It's always nice to have something to look forward to, isn't it?

PASSIVE VS ACTIVE WRITING

Ooh, I love this! It's one of my favourite strategies for making writing *Simply Irresistible*. And yes, I'm doing *that* dance as I write this. And no, if you don't know what I'm talking about you're not forgiven. Google it.

Anyhoo, passive versus active writing is a much-lauded yet much angst-causing writing convention. It's a by-product of academic writing, no doubt about it and as highlighted by Don Watson's chagrin regarding weasel words, it's the preferred style of bureaucrats because of its ability to slow down and chunk up sentences.

Put simply, and by way of one of my favourite writing rule books, *The Elements of Style* by Strunk and White, the impact of writing with an active voice is a piece that is 'more direct and vigorous than the passive.' Direct and vigorous for the win! *The Australian Style Manual* backs this up: 'There will be times when the passive is the only suitable consecution but remember that misuse of the passive to produce deliberate ambiguity may antagonise readers.' I'm antagonised just reading this!

Sometimes, people can't see the difference between active and passive writing until they're shown it. So what is the difference?

The goal for brand writing is understanding and connection. This means focus must stay where we want it to land. When you think about how a sentence is constructed (be still my beating heart!), where the main focus of a sentence is usually its subject, the impact of active or passive voice becomes clear. It's about performing an action vs being the recipient of an action. I don't want to get too nerdy on you (OK, I do, but my editor won't let me), so here's the best way of showing the difference:

The cat sat on the mat. Active. Cat (subject), sat (verb), mat (subject).

vs

The mat was sat on by the cat. Passive. The mat is being acted upon. Unacceptable! Want some more examples, taken directly off my LinkedIn feed?

Before:

The goal of the program is to bring together women from all areas of marketing with the aim of building a genuinely supportive community and a safe space to talk about challenges and solutions.

After:
My program gathers women from across marketing, building a genuinely supportive, safe community to share challenges and solutions.

The other reason passive voice rears its ugly head is because of ye olde apostrophe, specifically where to stick it. People seem to believe that the apostrophe has a personal vendetta against them, which is how I feel about humidity. These are people who, rather than write 'the dog's breakfast,' write 'the breakfast of the dog.' The end result? A slab of copy that, funnily enough, is a dog's breakfast!

So, what's the rule? As per the clever Victorian School Mistress, an apostrophe shows the owner of anyone's things, and it's also useful for shortenings. Possession and contraction, right? Write the word that owns something and add an apostrophe and an s, but not in pronouns, inanimate objects or just to add to the confusion, Australian place names.

DETAILS, DETAILS, DETAILS

One of the reasons I find LinkedIn in particular such a slog is the sheer lack of storytelling across so much of my feed. While I don't believe LinkedIn or any of the platforms are the space for paragraph upon paragraph of Tolstoy-esque writing, a smidge of painting a picture through words wouldn't go astray. This is where details turn a fact into a story, and we do this through writing!

Fiction writers are lucky buggers—they have so many tools at their disposal to make words sizzle. They're also generous—there's very little reason brand writers can't commandeer their tools to do our own shouty-shouty via the wordy-words. One of the tools that non-fiction, aka business writers, don't use enough is bringing words to life through sensory detail. Details are incredibly important to evocative, compelling writing. 'Give things the dignity of their names.' And so say all of us, but specifically Natalie Goldberg in *Writing Down the Bones: Freeing the Writer Within*. In practice, this could look like taking 'The event included lunch,' and transforming it into a FOMO-inducing plate of copy such as, 'I was there for the connections but I stayed for the food. Picture my body weight in cheese and tiny little quiches looking like something straight out of Alice in Wonderland.'

That said, be a bit choosy when it comes to how you use detail. We want interesting; we don't want banal and we really don't want cheesy. Don't go for the obvious such as describing the sea as glittering or the thunder as crashing. Be adventurous but don't overreach. Remember the key of writing for a brand is clarity and connection. 'The writer takes the reader's hand and guides him through the valley of sorrow and joy without ever having to mention those words.' Natalie Goldberg again.

Details are a way to enable or facilitate that connection and to influence a reaction. The perfect example of this is a day at the beach. We all have in our own mind a picture of what the beach looks like but we all have a different beach in mind. For me, it's the wildness of an open surf beach in

South Gippsland. For others it's the millpond of Port Phillip Bay. I'd like you to control the image and not let people come up with their own idea about a place based on what they know—we want them to see your version, your view of something, in this case the beach. Share the things that you notice when you arrive at that destination. It might be the smell of something, or the way the sky looks, the sounds that you hear. Is it noisy? Is it quiet? Is it creepy quiet or serenely quiet? A sweltering hot day or a cold, grey one? Get away from the big picture and go into the detail, the small things that you might notice that other people might not. This is what makes writing fresh and vibrant and it's only natural that the senses come out to play.

As you write, think about how you can incorporate your five senses, the memorable sights, smells, tastes, sensations and sounds. The small details that are important to you will create a unique feel to your work, which makes it come alive for your reader. While it's not always possible or appropriate to pump our blog posts, email campaigns and social media captions full of the five senses, a sprinkling of a couple of them is rarely a bad idea. Sight doesn't always have to be a blanket description of something that spells out the colours and dimensions. It can include textures, light and movement. Scent doesn't have to be a fact or a simile—rather than writing something such as, 'smells like peppermint' (a simile) it can describe the response or the atmosphere, using descriptions such as warm, fresh, clean, stale, heavy. If you really want to show off, bring out the metaphors! And so on, through taste, touch and sound.

That fear of sounding boring that so many people shared with me in my survey? It's this down and dirty detail that gets us feelin' all the feels—emotions, am I right? Emotions really pack a punch to writing and they just pair so beautifully with sense and detail. It's much more powerful for the reading experience to read a description of an emotion than to simply name it. For example, fear is four little letters, but what does fear *feel* like? What does it look like? Rather than using the words, 'I felt frightened,' describe the way your body reacted to that fear. Was your heart racing? Did you feel a flush of heat across your face? Did you have the urge to run for the hills? A five-minute exercise I share in my writing programs is for people to write the name of an emotion in the middle of a blank page, and then in the spaces all around it write all the associations with that feeling. Use all your senses and try and capture some memories of times you felt that emotion.

Or, take a short cut and grab yourself an emotion thesaurus. This is a writer's best mate and is always pounced upon by people at my writing retreats.

You know what all this talk of senses, emotions and details is leading me to, don't you? Oh yes, I'm going there! Brace yourselves.

Show, don't tell. Yeah, yeah, I get it, you're fighting the urge to throw this book across the room. Good one, Holly. Show, don't tell; ugh, I've never heard that one before! There's a reason show, don't tell is as ubiquitous as 'You're on mute,' and that's because the pleasure behind reading is about painting that internal picture in our mind, guided by the author. How many times have you left a movie grumbling, 'Meh, not as good as the book, was it?' At the crux of things, writing is about enabling discovery. To inform, you just need information and facts, but to *engage*, you need detail and texture. It's about providing an experience through words. Chekov nailed the difference between showing and telling when he said: 'Don't tell me the sun is shining, show me the glint of light on broken glass.' Here's some examples:

I'm 49 and my life is unpredictable, yet fulfilling.
vs
As I drag my 49-year-old self through the supermarket, one daughter messages me to say she needs to be in the CBD by midday, my other daughter has lost her blazer and the dog has vomited. I rearrange my afternoon schedule to accommodate all of the above and can't help but smile.

Another one?
It was hot in the Queensland sun.
vs
Walking down a Brisbane city street I felt my scalp prickle as sweat rolled down my temple.

Shall we put this one into practice? Grab one of your recent social media captions and add a few spicy touches to the copy. And yes, 'a spicy touch' is a perfect example of what I mean!

VOICE AND SOUNDING LIKE YOU, NOT ME

When I ask a client 'What are we writing here?' I'm going back to what I always bang on about. Purpose and intent. At the crux of things, communications is all about taking a message and delivering it in a way that ensures the intended recipient receives it loud and clear. Brand writing, therefore, becomes critically important in landing that message. This is where tone and voice really come into play.

One of the issues that came up repeatedly in my mini-research piece was the question of authenticity and finding voice. Voice is an interesting concept. The only way a voice can be aligned is through a deep understanding of brand and the audience. Is your brand conversational or more formal? Is it colloquial or conservative? Is there a particular vernacular that's uniquely you, your brand, your industry and your audience? For example, it's relatively appropriate for staff at a juice bar to call their teenage customers babe. My pharmacist calling me 'babe?' Not so aligned. A brand that's all about credible expertise such as a mechanical engineer building bridges with an audience of fellow engineers, civil law experts and environmental science won't have 'bae,' 'slay' or 'hey there!' in their vernacular. Nay. This I pray. OK, I'll stop now, but do you get where I'm going here? The way language delivers a message influences a response. One might say it sways. OK, now I'll really stop.

> 'Common tools go on top. The commonest of all, the bread of writing, is vocabulary. In this case, you can happily pack what you have without the slightest bit of guilt and inferiority. As the whore said to the bashful sailor, "It aint how much you've got, honey, it's how you use it."'
>
> ~ Stephen King

King shares some beautiful examples about how different writers have effectively used vocabulary and language to connect and light up their work. What I really love about the diversity of the examples is the lack of judgement. He doesn't denounce language that is complicated or complex, nor does he overly praise the use of sparse, simple language. Both have their place. In the context of writing for your brand, there may be cause for you to dig deep on your multi-syllable words that the average Jane can't grab. If you're the aforementioned engineer writing for other engineers, then go for it. Go technical! If you're an engineer writing for the people who will be beneficiaries or users of your technology, write in a way that allows them to access your expertise.

In the simplest of terms, voice is achieved through writing like you speak, and in a way that your audience can access. Thus, voice isn't just what you say, but it's also how you say it. It needs to be a fit for your brand and for your audience. The language, expressions and turns of phrases that you'd use if your brand was in the surfing industry targeting adolescents is completely different to that of a marriage celebrant targeting baby-boomers celebrating love late(r) in life.

Voice isn't always easy to bring to life in the writing process, but it's something that is almost criminally easy to bring to the editing process. Look at your writing and add as many contractions as humanly possible. This might be such as changing instructions such as 'Do not do this' to 'Don't do it!' Cut out any passive sentences. Use words you actually speak every day. For example, nothing grinds my gears like people writing a bland sentence like, 'I enjoy participating in team sports.' Instead, try this: 'Every weekend, you'll find me belting up and down a basketball court dreaming I'm LeBron.' Just like a personal stylist might give you a little sparkly something to add some zhoosh to an outfit, so too with language. Sprinkle power words like glitter. These are a set of words that copywriters use, particularly in ad-land, as they are proven to elicit a response. Email me and I'll shoot you through a set. Some are borderline ridiculous for many brands (I'm looking at you, 'badass') but others can lift a headline or an introduction from the merely meh to the swoon-worthy. And yes, swoon-worthy is a designated power word. Write your first draft, then in the rewrite add spunk and personality via swapping around words.

A tiny caveat: writing like you speak is advice that's thrown around quite a bit, and I prescribe to it to a degree. So much about writing is unlocking our own voice and our own style. However, sometimes we have nuances in the way we speak that simply don't make sense in writing. They just don't. What is quirky, engaging and endearing in person becomes impenetrable or simply annoying in writing. I never advocate for mixing metaphors, but I have a beautiful friend for whom mixing metaphors is as much a part of who she is as her eyes or her hair. It's not unusual for Mills to nod wisely in response to something I'm venting about to tell me that 'A fish rots not far from the tree.' Would I want to read this in her 'About' page? Not especially.

Funny weird, or funny ha-ha? People often come to me wanting to have more humour in their public personas via their writing. They feel that their writing lets them down and doesn't show either their true nature or the diversity of their personality. They are credible, accomplished people, but their writing portrays them as boring and overly serious. I know how limiting this can feel, that you're presenting a dull, shadow version of yourself. When I travelled to Italy in my early thirties (I had my 31st birthday in bella Roma, in fact) I felt like I was overly earnest and fun-free. The effort to understand and be understood in a foreign language meant I stripped all of my quirks from the way I spoke, and couldn't rely on language for nuance. My ordinarily pun-tastic self struggled a bit.

Some brands just don't align to funny. They can do warm and accessible, but funny might be too much of a stretch. Of course, there are sliding scales of funny and sometimes the only way to see if it works is to try it, but always remember the context of your audience and message. If you want to give a sense of trust and warmth to someone feeling vulnerable, such as the feel of a coffee chat with a good friend, humour is a great way to inject that vibe. For every new client project, I ask people to complete a brand story questionnaire where I ask for a few bits and bobs about their brand and about their project. A client came to me ahead of launching a new service, and this specific project was about cleaning up some mixed and messy messages on a website.

My survey asks the question: What are we going to be creating together?

The answer, perhaps my favourite in the decades I've been doing this work:

'Clarity. Does my ask look big in this?'

It's a simple tweak to a well-known colloquialism which had me snort-laughing coffee across my keyboard. It's clever, funny and in line to this specific brand, which is all about vibrant, fun, accessible self-leadership, yet the website was full of stilted, formal language with no sense of joy. You can bet your whatever-is-most-dear-to-you that I added a metric crap-ton of personality to her messages!

Here's an example of voice in action:

Before:
Blue51 Communications will be closed from Friday 1 October to Friday 9 November. Your email will be responded to from Monday 12 November.

After:
From Friday 1 October I shall be swapping my Word Nerd/ Blue51 adventures for three weeks of making memories with my family, whether they like it or not. I'll get back to you when I'm back on deck on Friday 9 November, which is also when green smoothies will be back on the menu.

Here's an example of an Instagram caption from a property brand targeting home buyers:

Before:
This property has an arrival that calms and rejuvenates. Our latest addition is about to launch in the heart of Suburb X—eight curated homes, landscaped gardens and flexible contemporary office space with onsite cafe. Conceived, designed and built by Builder X. The beautiful choreography of people and space.

After:

Welcome home! Our newest addition is about to launch smack bang in the middle of Suburb X, with eight beautifully designed and built homes, extensive landscaped gardens and a flexible, contemporary office space complete with cafe and the world's best banana bread.

See what I did there? The first caption feels as though it's speaking to the brand's colleagues, whereas the second one is pitched to the people who will actually purchase from the brand. The audience for this brand is people who want to live in an urban area evocative of their ideal lifestyle and love where they live. In this copy tweak I've gone for a voice where the brand punches 'em in the throat with its charming personality.

FORM AND FUNCTION

Good writing flows or moves in a way that's logical, easy, and seamless for the reader. This is constructed through correct grammar, the order of information, the rhythm and pace of what we write as well as through thoughtful use of devices and techniques. Hello, storytelling!

There are a couple of storytelling structures that I simply love pinching from the realm of fiction for my brand writing for clients.

Goal, motivation and obstacle are three little words that pack a storytelling sucker punch by way of an old-school structure:

Goal—what you want
Motivation—why you want it
Obstacle—what's in the way

Here's an example from fiction:

Goal—Charlie wants a golden ticket.
Motivation—A visit to the chocolate factory provides a life-changing opportunity to break the shackles of poverty.
Obstacle—Charlie's poverty means his chances of winning a ticket are zilch.

Here's an example from brand storytelling:

Goal—A person wants to feed their family nutritious, delicious wholefoods made from scratch.
Motivation—This will enhance their children's health and vitality.
Obstacle—The machine to make their goal a reality costs more than $2K.

See how clearly and beautifully this could roll out in a piece of content? In that business example (that I whipped up as easily as a green smoothie) the next couple of paragraphs would demonstrably share how to overcome that obstacle of cost, such as an interest-free payment feature and cost savings over time.

Another old-school approach that connects like the afore-mentioned sucker punch to the kisser is The Hero's Journey.

'The Hero's Journey is an incredibly tenacious set of elements that springs endlessly from the deepest reaches of the human mind; different in its details for every culture, but fundamentally the same.'

~ Christopher Vogler, *The Writer's Journey*

It's a rare content plan of mine that doesn't include some form of case study. They're also often the cause of a smidge of consternation. Case study? With annotations and citations? With data and hypotheses and qualitative and quantitative and lions and tigers and bears, oh my? Relax, no.

When I talk case study, I mean showcasing the work you do in context. Easy peasy—particularly when it incorporates one of the most popular (and effective, which is why it is so popular!) fiction structures ever in the history of telling stories—aka The Hero's Journey. You'll recognise The Hero's Journey from your favourite books and movies. 'But isn't The Hero's Journey for *Die Hard*, not *Finance is Us*?' I hear you cry? Well, let's just say I've repurposed The Hero's Journey just like I've (single-handedly) brought sexy back. It's no less of a fabulous tool for brand storytelling, too. As Chris Vogler explains, 'In any good story the hero grows and changes, making a journey from one way of being to the next: from despair to hope, weakness to strength, folly to wisdom, love to hate, and back again. It's these emotional journeys that hook an audience and make a story worth watching.' The basic structure I've modified for my Blue51 brand of case study storytelling is person, problem, my approach to solving it and the solution.

Here's an example of the bare bones hero's journey in the context of a career coach:

Introduction to the hero of the story: i.e. a client not feeling their most vibrant self at work and examples of how that manifested: boredom, anxiety, procrastination, disconnection from their work, working just to pay the bills.

Inciting incident: what made them decide enough's enough and reach out to you? What was their breaking point?

Your solution: i.e. how working with you addressed the issues you raised in the introduction. This could include testimonials or hard data from the person, i.e. "After working with me, Holly said she is now excited for what each day will bring!"

Conclusion—this is your Call To Action, basically where you say, "You can have the same feeling as Holly, so book a chat with me now."

> 'Stories built on the model of the Hero's Journey have an appeal that can be felt by everyone, because they well up from a universal source in the shared unconscious and reflect universal concerns.'
>
> ~ Christopher Vogler again.

This is connection and what I really, *really* love about this hero's journey approach to case studies is that it banishes that obstacle to writing that so many people have: sharing and showcasing their smarts without feeling like a dickhead. Yes, that's a direct quote.

So where to kick off?

'Where shall I begin, please your Majesty?' he asked. 'Begin at the beginning,' the king said, gravely, 'and then go on till you come to the end: then stop.'
~ Lewis Carroll, *Alice's Adventures in Wonderland*

The beginning is the most important piece of the writing, and is what makes a reader decide to keep on reading or to scroll on by. On that note, whomever is telling people to kick off, well, anything, with 'According to the Oxford Dictionary...' please stop. Not only is it boring to read (and probably to write) and completely unimaginative, the good ole Oxford isn't even the Australian publishing industry dictionary of choice. We Aussies are Macquarie all the way, baby!

Now that I've got that off my chest, a beginning isn't the easiest of things to write but thanks to the magic of the rewrite (more on that soon) they're possibly the easiest bit to fix after the first draft. When you're looking at a whole rather than a sum of parts, it's easier to see if there's something in the middle that would make a better beginning, and vice versa.

Like all brand writing, let's go with thinking about what we want by way of outcome. Consider how you want your readers to respond emotionally to your introduction: shocked, surprised, seduced, inspired, heard? Either way, let's make them feel *something*.

Writing doesn't have to be chronological. Decide on the order or flow that best suits the piece and the reader. Relate the information in whatever permeation you like. This is where stealing from fiction can really come into its own; what's a narrative structure that best suits this information? Is it a hero story or a three act arc? Is it a reverse pyramid, as used by journalists for news stories? This is a descending hierarchy where the most important, newsworthy, must-know information is at the top followed by the less important background information. A services page, for example, will have the reverse structure where the investment is below all the colour and texture and excitement-building copy that makes the price irrelevant. Just sign me up already!

I had a wonderful lecturer in my Writing and Literature MA who was a self-described movie buff. Everything he read led to him imagining how it would open as a movie. One of his techniques for more interesting writing was to apply that idea to anything and everything he wrote. In his class, Creative Non-fiction, I wrote a profile piece on a farmer. Here's the facts: he was a multi-generational farmer who made his living growing seasonal produce. He experienced times of feast and famine in terms of cashflow. He was quietly spoken and according to my notes, it was shaping up to be a pretty bloody boring profile. I had no real grasp on how I was going to start the piece with enough spark for anyone to keep reading. One point of interest in my notes? Three mornings a week, together with his wife, he left their farm at 3 am in their old banger of a truck to take their produce to a wholesale market in the heart of the city. Imagine this as a movie—headlights cutting through the darkness of an empty highway, the glow of the city faint in the far distance, his wife asleep on his shoulder, Roy Orbison playing softly over the rattle of the crates of produce bouncing in the truck bed behind him. Isn't that a much more compelling way to share some information? The only thing missing is the all-pervading eau de fertiliser emanating from his clothes.

Another example of this comes by way of one of the incredible members of my Band of Batchers. Jaqui is an ultra-runner who spends a lot of time in the Aussie bush running remarkable distances—I'm talking hundreds of kilometres across days and nights. After every event, Jaqui writes an event report which I eagerly await. In one of Jaq's reports, she had a chronological structure that included all the details of the event, from the time she took off until she crossed the finish line in the early hours of the next day. I share this example with Jaqui's permission:

Before:
The weather was looking ideal and after six months training, the anticipation had kicked in as we packed up the car and hit the road on Friday. I was never more organised for a race, with each aid station's bag packed with food and clothing and maps printed and laminated.

After:
The air felt like ice with every breath. The fog had cleared, and the stars were lighting my way as I pushed my feet through mud, kilometre after kilometre. Through the fog, eyes glowed in the dark ahead of me. Suddenly two eyes became a hundred. I stopped breathing...

Fancy one more example?

While I'd never in a million years suggest that a mortgage broker's content is boring, some of the pieces I see on ye olde internet don't really light me up. Tell me, what grabs your interest most out of the following two lines:

Buyer understanding of existing mortgage rates is negligible.

OR

97% of home owners are locked in to the wrong mortgage rate—and they don't even know it.

Yep. Me too. *Nips off to check mortgage rate*

TURNING WORD VOMIT INTO BRAND WRITING GORGEOUSNESS

Congratulations! You've taken the blank page and with a rapid fire tap, tappity, tap, you have sprinkled it with content destined to hit your intended reader right in the chops. Now it's time to triumphantly trash a hotel room, then put your feet up and relax. Or is it? Spoiler alert: it's not. Now we need vigilance. Now we review the writing to make it tighter, more effective, more engaging, something you're proud of. Now we step into the rewriting or revision process. Ah, my favourite. This is where we give a shit, as I so poetically expressed earlier.

Sometimes the terms revision, rewriting and editing are interchanged, which causes some confusion as well as much consternation from the likes of yours truly. The confusion is warranted—there are multiple types of editing within the broader definition, such as structural edit, line edit and copy edit. For the purposes of this book, of writing for your brand, we're going to use rewrite and revision interchangeably, while we'll limit the concept of editing to the grammar and spelling/nuts and bolts element of getting your work ready for the world.

My clients know that as they write a first draft, I encourage them to write, write, write and let it all out. For the second draft, aka the rewrite, I encourage them—and you, dear reader—to calm the farm!

'Writing is rewriting' is an ethos or a philosophy that's trotted out by luminaries aplenty—everyone from Zadie Smith, Truman Capote and Earnest Hemingway. Hemingway also infamously advised, 'Write drunk, edit sober.' This is something I always struggle with. I understand that the cold, hard light of rationalism needs to be applied against the almost magical energy of a first draft, but I don't see it as a 'sober' exercise in that I find myself just as alight during the revision or rewrite as I do during the first draft. It's still a creative process but now we get critical and a touch belligerent. The rewrite or revision is about transforming your first draft into well-considered, highly polished copy. Some writers believe the first draft is the easy part, akin to kids running wild at a birthday party, while the revision and edit is the clean-up. Others believe the first draft is the word vomit, and the real magic/writing happens in the rewrite. Honestly? I believe that it's a mix of the two. Even the most prolific and experienced writers in the world rarely get it right first go. A rewrite can feel as extensive as a first draft, which can feel overwhelming and off-putting to many writers, but for me? I bloody love the rewrite process. It's no less playful and creative and thought-provoking as the first draft. In fact, it allows more opportunity for creativity and word wrangling as you have a wonderfully solid scaffold to play off. You've done the hard yakka with the first draft, now is when you get to add the glitter, the writerly tricks and strategies. Don't get disheartened because this is where the magic happens.

But first—go for a trot around the block before you get buck naked for a read through, and take some deep breaths, because it could get gnarly. This is where I tell myself (and my clients) we're going to rip apart the work. It can be painful and difficult and so it's important to add a reminder not to be unkindly critical and never personal. We're looking at your writing here, not your inherent worth! We're aiming for some more objectivity.

It's really important to have some time and distance between finishing a first draft of anything and then getting back into it. I rarely write and publish a blog post on the same day. When I write content for clients, I allow space in my schedule for me to leave it for a few days while I work on other projects, then come back to it with fresh eyes. That first read through after the break is where I spot everything from embarrassingly obvious typos through to structural problems or voice wobbles.

On reading your work—this is when some of those inner 'mean editor' messages sidle their way into your head. While it is important to be critical while reading, it's quite a precarious line between thinking 'This line could do with some tightening up,' and 'Ugh, this is such crap!' Sometimes, we're so close to something that we think it's amazing, or the polar opposite. Be critically constructive. We're looking for improvement rather than the perfection that, firstly, leads to paralysis and secondly, doesn't exist.

You don't have to be literally naked—especially if you're in Melbourne. That's a sure-fire path to frostbite and you don't need that. By 'naked' read through I mean without undue fiddling, without making notes, without scribbling on your work. You're going to pick up that piece of writing and read it in one sitting if possible, as a reader, not as a writer, and definitely not as *the* writer. If you really, really can't help yourself, have a pen with you, and in the margins put a scribbled star against areas that vary between meh and bad, and a love heart next to the sections that are freakin' fabulous.

Read aloud! Some people like to get their writing program to read work to them but that separates the writer from the writing. When you read your work your tongue will almost literally tangle up in any clumsy expressions, whereas your ears might skip over it. You'll find any interruptions to the flow as well as any gaps. Listen for any clunkiness in the language, any words that don't sound right or don't feel right. Listen to the shape of your words, how well they roll off the tongue, how well each line works and whether they combine to make a well-rounded whole. If it feels clunky or hard to get out, if you're gasping for breath, it might mean your sentences are too long or need breaking up or restructuring. In reading aloud, you'll find wobbles and repetition that's either purposeful or accidental yet ultimately impactful, or irritating habits you'd overlooked. Me? I'm a shocker for 'and then', 'actually,' and 'in fact' when I'm writing, so they're three phrases that I always look for in my read-through. We all have nuances and the tongue will pick them up more effectively than the ear.

So, buck naked read complete, what were your reactions as a whole to what you've just read? Did it make sense overall? Are there any gaps or vital pieces of information missing? Is there too much detail that makes it overwhelming or impenetrable? Did you want to keep reading? What were the strengths of what you've just read? What did you really like? What stood out? What are you really proud of? On the flipside, were there any mehs? Were there any God-awfuls? Were there parts that were a bit confusing or boring? Hint—if you found yourself googling the average lifespan of a hairless cat it might be a sign that it doesn't sufficiently capture attention.

Some more specific questions to ask yourself are; does it flow? Is the focus right? Is there unnecessary fluff? Do you have the right mix of research and facts to back up your words? Are there any gaps or anything that's been left out? Does the ending and the transitions make sense and create a gorgeously readable flow? Is it engaging and interesting?

In the next read through we get down and dirty. Now, we scribble. Arm yourself with pens and dive into the detail of your writing, make observations and assessments, as coldheartedly as possible. What's the point of this sentence? This paragraph? Have I made it strong enough? Too strong? Is it even in the right place?

Ask yourself what's working, what doesn't work, what can be killed—and if so, stick a big line through anything that needs to be sent straight back to the hell from whence it came! Or, if it doesn't warrant outright banishment, circle it and write transfer in the margin. You'll figure out where later. Look for consistency and logic of ideas. Is the focus right? Is there any unnecessary repetition? Are the sentence lengths varied? Are the tone and language right overall as well as appropriate for the relevant audience?

What about any gaps in your information? Are there stories you can include to confirm or clarify your message, or just to deliver it in a more palatable way? What writerly strategies and devices can you apply to bring it to life? Play around with alternative positioning of paragraphs or sentences. Is the voice bang on? Is the ending right? Does it lead the reader to a predetermined (by you!) feeling?

Now, stick some ginger in your green smoothie for the rewrite. As you rewrite, you will be bringing your words to life, creating a beautiful whole. This is where you add your sensory details as we talked about in the sections on Life mapping and Details, details, details. Visual is always the most obvious, but beyond the memorable sights, can you bring in smells, tastes, sounds?

Finished your rewrite? Do a quick jig, and then sit yourself back down in front of your screen—it's copyediting time! Whoot whoot! Now is the time to fix pesky typos, check spelling, confirm all names, titles and details, and clean up grammar. You don't have to do this off a printed copy, reading off your screen can be fine, but regardless, again read your work aloud. Don't use the transcriber built in to your word processing software; use your voice.

CUT THE FLUFF!

'In English, as in all languages presumably, there are many powerful words. These words cannot be crowded together. They must be given a lot of space, room to breathe. Otherwise, like roosters in a cage, they'll peck each other to death.'

~ John Marsden

Rambling on was one of the obstacles to writing that people shared in my survey. So too was finding a way to convey the importance of a concept to their oblivious audience. These led people to overwrite, to either use jargon, technical or formal language, rather than carefully selected words that bring impact, sans padding. Marsden, continuing in the book *Everything I Know about Writing* referenced above, uses the example of 'Jesus wept.' This is the shortest verse in the English version of the Bible. Here's where I must confess that I thought 'Jesus wept!' was an Irish version of FFS. Oops, but both present a compelling case for powerful simplicity in language. Brevity and clarity is infinitely more appealing and influential.

'Working in with the concrete nouns are the verbs, those powerful words that form the spine and the movement of your prose. You don't need to strive for fancy verbs, just be alert to the presence of your verbs, and to the strength they lend the writing.'

~ Carmel Bird

I freaking love this advice! The only way to bring it to your work is to go ahead and take Stephen King's advice and 'kill your darlings.' Cull, cull, cull!

We're working towards economy, clarity and colour. Get rid of crappy language that serves no purpose. I'm talking using big words that are not only unnecessary, but are often contextually incorrect. No, they don't make you look clever. So too, super-long sentences. This is where you wander into the realm of waffle. Waffles for breakfast? Yeah, maybe. Waffle in writing for your brand? Hard pass! Long, complex sentences do little to enhance clarity and connection. If someone has to read and reread a social media caption to make sense of what you're trying to say, you've lost them, and they'll be less likely to stop the scroll next time your status update appears in their feed. Instead of waffle, let's aim for flow. Varied sentence lengths and structure will give that flow and will make it interesting.

Want to see brevity in action?

Before:
XYZ Dance Academy provides an environment that is inclusive of all students and fosters a love of Dance and Drama for both recreation and vocation. XYZ Dance Academy offers classes Monday to Saturday for 2 year olds to adults. Beginner to advanced skill levels.

After:
XYZ Dance Academy inspires a love of dance and drama in everyone. We're inclusive and have classes for tiny tots

through to adults, beginners as well as experienced dancers, for fun and fitness as well as performance and competition.

The 'after' has five words less than the 'before' which isn't earth-shattering, but each word now stands alone, uncrowded and unpecked. The grammar's pretty good, too!

Also be on alert for overwriting or Year 9 essay-style stilted writing, like this glorious example found in my letterbox despite my 'no advertising' sticker:

Before:
Dear Homeowner,
If you are giving consideration to selling in the near or far future, please find overleaf our Key Auction Dates Calendar to provide assistance to you in proceeding to plan your sale. Of additional support to homeowners over the next week we will be offering an opinion of value of homes in the area. If you would like to take advantage of this exciting opportunity to have your home appraised please contact me.

After:
Are you considering selling your home? March is a great time to sell! We're going to be in your neighbourhood next week and would love to have a chat with you about the market value of your home. Send me an email or give me a buzz to lock it in—contact details below.

Tautologies are the perfect way to piss off a word nerd as well as add unnecessary bulk. They are words that unnecessarily repeat, and their natural habitat seems to be LinkedIn updates. Here's a shocker of an example I found in my feed:

It's one of those invisible roadblocks that you can't see.

Really? You can't see something invisible?

George Orwell, author of *Animal Farm* and *1984* fame is reported to have written by the rule; 'If you can cut a word out, cut it out.' I do love this concept for its simplicity, but it might not always be applicable day-to-day when writing for your brand. Look, the stylistic advice given against adverbs in creative and non-fiction writing is to lose them. I'm talking words like very, just, really, absolutely, extremely. As qualifiers, they make words lose their individual power, diluting the impact and, subsequently, meaning. Less is more, and all that. I get it; adverbs, qualifiers or modifiers add weight and word count. However, when writing for a brand our focus is broader than readability. We're looking for relatability and beautiful, compelling communications. We're looking for ways to convey brand persona, a sense of usefulness and authority. So, when used judiciously, adverbs also add depth, personality and warmth, which is essential to conversational writing, which converts readers to fans to clients. Conversational writing fosters connection, which is the whole name of the game when it comes to writing for a brand.

Let's have a look at an adverb used to effect:

Before:
It was absolutely the most humiliating moment of my career.

Does this sentence need the 'absolutely'? Probably not, because we have words like 'humiliating' and 'most' right next to each other which implies the absolutely. Let's pack more of a punch:

After:
Was it the most humiliating moment of my career? Absolutely!

Bottom line—kill your darlings, and don't be stingy when it's time to cull your work. Always keep your audience, message and purpose front of mind. Cull in the context of what's going to be the most efficient and effective way to link your audience to your message.

STARING DOWN THE BLANK PAGE

So, you're ready to sit at your desk and write some fabulous copy that's going to utterly dazzle your reader with your message. You have ideas up the wahzoo, you've ordered your ideas into a format that makes sense—now it's time to write! This is where the brain can quite inexplicably freeze and you can suddenly be overcome by an urge to clean the skirting boards around your house, by hand, with a toothbrush. Gah!

This isn't writer's block—you know what you want and need to write. Let's just think of it as a vintage car that needs a bit of a warm up or a running start.

One of the beautiful yet infuriating things about writing is there are as many different approaches as there are writers. *Making Stories* by Kate Grenville and Sue Woolfe is an interesting left-of-centre craft book that details how ten Australian novels were written. It includes author interviews and writer notebook extracts to tell the story of how some of my favourite books came to life. What blows me away is that while there were some overlaps in process, each author had a different approach to moving from a blank page to a completed work. Some start at their version of 'Once upon a time' and keep on truckin' 'til they hit 'The End.' Others finish a writing session with an incomplete sentence (which would do my head in) so they start their next session with a very clear starting point. Others describe choosing quick and easy sections that they can rapidly bang out to get that endorphin and productivity-inducing hit that comes with momentum.

'Writing is an incremental process and often the increments don't come in a strictly chronological, beginning-to-end fashion, even if in the final draft that's the way a reader will encounter them.'

~ Robert Root

When I'm working with a client to write a larger project such as a book, they're often relieved when I share that they don't have to write their first draft chronologically following an outline. In fact, one of my clients wrote her book which was a blend of memoir and biography by alternating the more harrowing sections of her story such as her father's passing with a story that had her in tears of laughter, when as a teenager her father picked her up and put her in a rubbish bin in front of her crush. Some people like to start their first draft at the end of their book, rather than the very beginning. Some start at the beginning, or with a story anywhere in their outline that gives either the warm fuzzies or makes their blood boil. Basically, they pick a section and get stuck in!

Another fantastic way to get words flowing is to jump-start a writing session with a spot of free association writing. Sometimes known as Morning Pages, (a phrase coined by Julia Cameron in her seminal work, *The Artists Way*) this method is grounded in science and psychology as a way to warm up your writing muscles. It clears your head and focuses your thought. Here's some performance psychology babble: research suggests free association writing increases happiness and mental health. This comes from being in the zone and dumping the 60,0000 circling, contradictory, perplexing and confrontational thoughts many of us hold, cluttering up our mental space. Boom! People who free association write daily are also shown to have a stronger immune system due to the chemical response that releases dopamine. Boom boom!

Free association writing goes a little something like this:

Stop. Let your senses fall on something outside yourself. What can you see? Can you see flowers, a tree, the neighbour's filthy gutters? What can you hear? At any given time I can hear the dog snuffling. Other people might hear traffic, or the sound of the heater clicking on and off. What can you smell? The aroma of the coffee on your desk is just the start: think about its taste, the temperature, how you loved that little beachside cafe where you drank coffee as a gorgeous young thing in your twenties. Perhaps you're wondering where you left your keep cup?

Set a timer for ten minutes, pick up your pen and write, using the first sense that grabbed you as your starting point. Keep writing until the timer goes off and stop grumbling— Cameron prescribes thirty to forty minutes or three A4 pages, so I'm letting you off easy. If you go off on a tangent that's fine. If you get stuck and can't write, go back to what's in your direct line of sight. You can even incorporate your response: 'This is a waste of time, my head's all over the place,' but keep going. Note the emotions that arise. How is your body feeling? Write freehand without stopping, using full sentences and don't edit or rewrite as you go. If you find yourself judging, make note of it and keep going.

Free association writing makes you go deeper with your thoughts than usual, and clears your head to create space for deeper activity. It loosens you up and sometimes these sessions uncover a post, piece or an idea worth exploring. It unlocks the brain and your creativity before you get started with your 'real' writing for the day. If I'm ever feeling stuck and resistant to writing I'll set the alarm for ten minutes and scribble. That gets me over the 'not feelin' it' vibe.

> *'For I believe that eventually quantity will make for quality... Quantity gives experience. From experience alone can quality come.'*
>
> ~ Ray Bradbury

Free association writing fosters a habit and improves writing. I've set challenges with clients to free write every day for two weeks and the improvement in both their output and the quality of their writing is staggering.

Here's what's really key here; when it doubt, scribble it out. The power of free association writing is scientifically linked to handwriting. There's a freedom that comes with handwriting. There's more than a scant handful of authors who write their entire first drafts of significantly large books by hand. I'm cramping up just thinking about that, but almost nothing leaves my writing desk without first starting life as a scribble on a piece of paper. It's freeing and liberating. And it's science, y'all, which is why I only prescribe handwriting for the outlining process. The act of handwriting for outlining and for fleshing out ideas ahead of writing accesses different parts of the brain. The act of physically moving ideas across a page by hand is a way to both capture ideas but also expand upon them—you'll quickly find that as you move through this process the ideas will flow thick and fast.

When you step into your writing room (that feels beautifully Elizabethan, doesn't it, and you just know I'm imagining a quill here) you'll have outlines of your beautifully fleshed out ideas so you can just get stuck into the writing. All the thinking's pretty much done, so you can turn your outlines into content to engage your audience. You basically just write, filling in the gaps, turning all your dot point scribbles into sentences and paragraphs: all the good stuff.

FIND THE FLOW AND GETTING IT DONE

Flow is a wonderful thing—the writing takes over, the words dance across the page. You blink, and the word count extends into the thousands! However, reading back through the work you realise it's not what you intended. This is sometimes a good thing, but sometimes not. I wrote a piece for a client once that had the express purpose of showcasing their journey from wannabe through to formidable expert, definitely someone to know, like and trust. As I dug deep into their accomplishments the piece very quickly turned into something akin to the 21st birthday speech delivered by a semi—tipsy bestie. I'd lost the focus in all my enthusiasm in putting the spotlight on this person.

Turns out I'm not alone:

'I'm continually losing my way and losing confidence. You have a burst of excitement and think, I've got this; then a day later I'm in a mess, nothing's in control, I've lost focus. So I sit down and say, 'This is a story about...' Then I think, OK, that's something I can write.'

Peter Carey

My way back to focus is to remind myself of the purpose of the piece. What am I writing? Who's the audience? What do they need from this content? What do I need them to take from it? These questions guide me through the rewrite.

I have one sure-fire way to find that sweet space of flow, and there's no real eloquent way to say it other than to bang it out. The rough draft by its very name should be rough! The number one rule in my writing sessions (both my personal sessions as well as those I host for others) is to *keep writing*. Just keep going. If you're getting stuck make a couple of dot points or sentences about what you want as an outcome or what to include for this piece that's giving you grief and move on to the next section.

Bang it out, she says. It'll be easy, she says? But how?

Say hello to batch writing. It's a way to get a ton of content done and dusted ready for a quick sprinkle of writerly glitter via a revision process before it's shared with the world. It's time out of the Business as Usual and all the distractions to simply smash out your content and to knock off projects that have been lurking on your to do list for far too long.

I love batch writing. I've batch written for years. My favourite day in the office is when I'm writing up a storm, finishing the day feeling quietly smug that I have created a ton of content ready for a spit and polish. It's such a great way to get content out of your head and into the world. Batching means writing your content and telling your story without the angst. It's getting a first draft D.O.N.E. - done!

They say that when it comes to making a pavlova, the most critical success factor is a super clean bowl, an equally squeaky clean whisk and room temperature eggs. Likewise, the secret to a really successful batch writing session is preparation, minus the clean mixer and leaving eggs lying around on your bench. You see, my batch writing approach is to write in sprints over a period of time. This means that when I start each sprint, I need to have a fairly clear idea of what it is I'll actually be writing. I want the sprint to be pure writing time, not staring out the window conceptualising time. The best way to enable that is by having created detailed outlines in advance, handwritten, of course, as per the previous section.

Another way I get into flow is to dedicate a couple of hours or a day to having word wars with myself. I love, love, LOVE word wars—basically, I set a timer for 10 minutes, write like the clappers as my dear old dad would say and when the buzzer buzzes, I check my word count. Then I go again, but this time I'm aiming to beat that previous word count. I do this five times, and I could conceivably have written anything between 1,250 and 5,000 words in an hour. Over the course of the day? Tens of thousands of words. Insert smug face here!

Is there a big project you need to tackle, a book-sized project perhaps? Have a crack at a 90-90-1 approach. Every day for the next 90 days, dedicate the first 90 minutes of each day to 1 goal. If you can't do weekends or specific days (such as Christmas or your cherub's birthday) add that time, and spread it equally across the days you can do. It's a fabulous way to focus and GSD consistently and in the context of writing your book this strategy can be used repeatedly across the different elements such as outlining and research, first draft completion and then revising and editing.

If 90 minutes isn't possible, tweak the formula to 60-60-1 to get your work over the line. Fun fact—I did a sprint of one hour a day for 56 days to complete my novel's second draft and where I missed a couple of days I added those missed hours to the following weekend to make sure each week I'd dedicated a minimum of 7 hours to my book. I have the chart to prove it!

Here's something I tell my clients All.The.Time. Writing a first draft of anything should be fun! Probably nobody will see your first draft and it's certainly not going to appear on a billboard, so let's treat it with all the joyful freedom it deserves. It's simply playing with words. It's moving ideas around. It's getting it out, banishing that blank page so you can move into the next stage, the best stage, where we add the writerly glitter and make a connection with words. This can only happen, the banging it out bit, when I've told my inner 'mean editor' to bugger off in no uncertain terms. It's not their time at the draft stage. Their time to shine will be in the revision process; the job of the first draft is purely to get it out. Grammar be damned! What's spelling? Bugger off, rules, conventions and standards. Step aside, stylistic choices. Mama's got a draft to bang out!

WRITING IS A PRACTICE

It's a very rare person I come across that, despite writing frequently and beautifully, actively and openly despises writing. Hello, Caroline! This is reinforced to me through the feedback that I receive after each and every batch writing workshop—it's an almost unanimous expression of surprise and gratitude for the reconnection to something that can give so much joy. It's also something that only gets better the more you do it, so it's well worth making it a practice.

> 'Like running, the more you do it, the better you get at it. Some days you don't want to run and you resist every step of the three miles, but you do it anyway. You practice, whether you want to or not. You don't wait around for inspiration and a deep desire to run... Once you're deep into it, you wonder what took you so long to finally settle down at the desk. Through practice you actually do get better.'
>
> ~ Natalie Goldberg

I'm a working writer, so I don't have time to lounge about, waiting for the muse to strike. Instead, my writing practice is scaffolded against rituals and routines I've carved out over time, which make writing almost as habitual as brushing my teeth, and they all start with knowing what it is I'm actually writing about. It's a working environment that's set up to support me—nothing gets my hackles up like reaching for the pad of sticky notes that are always to the left of my desk, only to find them in the possession of a certain light-fingered cherub that I brought into this world. That said, you may benefit from a change of scenery from time to time, and what works for one writer might not work for the next.

'In the end, there is no one ideal condition for creativity.'

~ Twyla Tharp

Hell, some writers change their setting for every new project!

One of the best things about writing for a brand is the structure that's inherent. We don't do scattergun, do we? No! We write strategically and intentionally. This is where a content planner really brings a brand alive, as it details the E.V.E.R.Y.T.H.I.N.G. involved in sharing a story. Of course, you can grab yourself a copy of my wonderful content planner, *Write Your Year*, but a notebook will do the trick. In fact, my planner is the meticulous zhooshing up of many years of notebooks. I do suggest, however, you get yourself a notebook with a fair bit of sturdiness to it; you're going to be spending a lot of time together! Make no mistake—I want you to deface the living shizzle out of your notebook. Ideally, after a year of solid writing planning it should be torn, coffee-stained and covered with sticky notes. You see, your notebook will be home to notes to self, tracking against goals, ideas for blog posts, emails and captions, prompts, words you like and words you dislike and don't want associated with your brand. If you're someone who likes to track your progress, you might like to spend five minutes after each writing session recording in your notebook what you achieved, including word count and what's planned for your next writing session.

Depending on how prolific you are, you might like to grab a document box or folder for your content. It doesn't have to be a literal box, but this incredibly important spoke in your marketing and branding wheel deserves a home for your ideas. I prefer boxes because they're more forgiving for the physical 'mess' of content. It's portable, so you can take it to a cafe or away to one of my writing retreats in coastal Victoria.

> *'I start every dance with a box. I write the project name on the box, and as the piece progresses I fill it up with every item that went into the making of the dance. This means notebooks, news clippings, CDs, videotapes of me working alone in my studio, videos of the dancers rehearsing, books and photographs and pieces of art that may have inspired me.'*
>
> ~ Twyla Tharp again.

Chapter Six

SOME FINAL WORDS

BUT I'M NOT CREATIVE...

If there's one line that makes me borderline weepy, it's this one. 'But I'm not creative.' I've had too many people confess that to me. It's just so limiting and patently untrue!

Writing for your brand is creative—it might be based on fact, sure, but the act itself is creative. It requires instinct, brain matter and a delicate dance between logic and imagination in conveying your expertise into a format that someone not so attuned to your knowledge can access. It benefits as much from a storytelling approach as does fiction. Sometimes, when I suggest some writing activities and challenges that clearly come from the creative writing camp I get a bit of push back. 'But I'm not writing a novel, Holly, I'm writing my sales page.' In response, here's something I tell my clients All.The.Time.: writing a first draft of anything should be fun!

Loosen up the creativity muscles with some fun, liberating writing exercises such as free association writing or a memory kickstart writing session. Remember the poetry fragments magnets that were everywhere in the late '90s? It wasn't just good for leaving filthy messages for people on the fridge, it was really good for unlocking creativity and for coming up with unexpected pairings of words. Get yourself a set, and play.

I hope I've shown you that the tools, techniques and approaches at the keyboards of fiction writers are often no less applicable than what you write for your LinkedIn posts. So, bring on the tools that fiction writers use every day in their craft. Most importantly—writing is an opportunity for creativity. The joy that unfolds from a creative act can't be underestimated. Creativity is a muscle and one that deserves flexing. Yes, this is me offering my full and abundant permission for you to go flex.

Go, write and be joyful!

NOT QUITE 'THE END'

I'd love to hear about your writing, so please reach out to me! I have an ever-evolving and growing collection of writing and communications wisdom on my website and I share my insights, writing events and communications tips and tricks with my mailing list each fortnight. I'd love you to jump aboard! You can join my list on my website and there are links from you-know-where to breakfast across my social media platforms.

Writing is a solo activity but you don't have to feel lonely—
I offer a range of ways to bust through that sense of professional
isolation, including my Band of Batchers group writing
program, my Write Here Right Now batch writing workshops
and my First Draft Fast Track program. If you'd like a little
more red pen action from me to get a book done and dusted,
my Book Lab program might be just the ticket! Please shoot
me an email at **hello@blue51.com.au** for more information.

Further reading

I almost didn't include this advice within these covers, but how could I possibly write a book about writing better without including the most fundamental building block? You ready for the pot of gold at the end of the rainbow? You sure? OK, here we go:

Writers read.

That's it. Writers read. I could share all the devices, strategies and techniques in the world, but that would mean nothing without seeing them in context, seeing how other writers have brought them to life. I encourage you to read widely, across many genres. Writing for your brand is relatively factual. It's not often making shit up, to be blunt, and so some examples of beautifully crafted non-fiction (or creative non-fiction as it was called in my master's studies) is worth reading.

Here's some of my favourites:

True Stories by Helen Garner, Text, 1996. Hell, read anything and everything Helen Garner!

The Faber Book of Reportage—this was a set text and my dad commandeered my copy over twenty years ago and I still haven't managed to get it back. Basically, it covers 'news' from the time of the Pharaohs through to the Gulf War. Please note: some of the mid-century pieces, particularly around the liberation of the concentration camps is particularly harrowing.

Best Australian Essays—these are annual anthologies that I scoop up whenever I spot them in second hand bookshops.

Australian Book Review—this is a magazine of great writing.

The Monthly—this journal features articles by some of the best writers, journalists and commentators in Australia.

Literary journals such as *Meanjin* and *Overland* are great additions to your reading repertoire. Not just non-fiction, they also feature poetry, short stories and book extracts.

If you'd like to check out my list of excellent books about the craft of writing, pop down to the next section titled 'A few of my favourite things.'

A few of my favourite things

Here's a non-exhaustive list of my favourite books about the craft of writing, some of which I've directly quoted in the pages of this book:

- *Ideas into Words: Mastering the Craft of Science Writing*, Elise Hancock, The John Hopkins University Press, 2003,
- *Media Writing: A Practical Introduction 2nd Edition*, Craig Batty and Sandra Cain, Macmillan Education, 2016
- *Writing the Story of Your Life: The Ultimate Guide*, Carmel Bird, Harpers Collins, 2007
- *The Seven Basic Plots: Why We Tell Stories*, Christopher Booker, Bloomsbury, 2004
- *Tell Your Story—build your brand and grow your business*, Holly Cardamone 2020
- *The Creative Habit: Learn it and use it for life*, Twyla Tharp, Simon & Shuster 2006
- *To Show and to Tell: The Craft of Literary Nonfiction*, Phillip Lopate, Free Press, New York, 2013

- *Writing Down the Bones: Freeing the Writer Within*, Natalie Goldberg 30th Anniversary Edition, Shamble Publications 2016
- *Drawing on the Right Side of the Brain 4th Edition*, Betty Edwards, 2012
- *The Artist's Way*, Julia Cameron, 1992
- *On Writing: A Memoir of the Craft*, Stephen King, Hoddor, 2000
- *Story Genius: How to use brain science to go beyond outlining and write a riveting novel*, Lisa Cron, Ten Speed Press, 2016
- *Media Writing: A practical Introduction* 2nd Edition, Craig Batty and Sandra Cain, Macmillan Education London, 2016
- *Zen in the Art of Writing*, Ray Bradbury, Harper Voyager, 1994
- *Style: Toward Clarity and Grace*, Joseph M. Williams, The University of Chicago Press, Chicago, 1990
- *Death Sentence: The decay of Public Language*, Don Watson, 2003
- *The Elements of Style*, Strunk and White
- *The Australian Style Manual*
- *Everything I Know about Writing*, John Marsden, Pan Macmillan, 1993
- *The Nonfictionists's Guide: On Reading and Writing Creative Nonfiction*, Robert Root, Rowman & Littlefield Publishers Inc, New York, 2008
- Peter Carey in *Making Stories: How ten Australian novels were written*, Kate Grenville and Sue Woolfe, Allen and Unwin, 2001

Acknowledgements

This book, my work and my writing life more broadly is the result of the incredible generosity of writers, authors, poets, lecturers, colleagues and friends sharing their thoughts about writing and the writing process over decades of conversations, conferences, workshops, lectures, festivals, tutorials, coffee catch ups, booze ups, articles, books and interviews. Decades, I'm telling you! This means that the people I'm grateful to, that I'm indebted to for writing and communications guidance, learning and insights—both deliberate and intentional as well as inadvertent and accidental—are far too many to recall, let alone name.

However, there are some I simply have to highlight:

My clients: your work inspires me every day. Every day! I cross paths with such inspiring people, experts in their field, making the world a better place. It never fails to blow me away that I'm the word nerd you trust to help you shine a spotlight on yourself and your work through my writing and communications services, programs, events and retreats. Through your stories I get to inhabit your world and your work. Regardless of what my clients do for a living, it makes an impact on me personally on many levels, be it through how I look at the contemporary world of work or, for a specific example, how I use a sticky note. Thanks Debbie Wood for simultaneously blowing my mind and changing my life by teaching me the inherent danger in peeling, not lifting.

My formidable Band of Batchers—we first 'gathered' in April 2020, and over the subsequent months and years, in and out of Melbourne lockdowns, we shared laughs, tears, celebrations, commiserations, content ideas and potato recipes. Three years later and I still get bouncy-excited each month when Band week rolls around. Love you batchers!

While this is a book about writing, content marketing takes many forms and it's a means by which wonderful humans have crossed my path. The people who bared their writerly souls in response to my survey came to me by way of LinkedIn and my email list. Steph Clarke dedicated an episode of her incredible podcast to *Tell Your Story*, where she described its impact on her as a way to not have boring brands. Steph, you inspired this book in general, and my subtitle more specifically and I can't wait to hear your three takeaways from this book!

Team Blue51: it takes a village, so they say, and not to brag, but my village is extraordinary. Thank you for keeping the engine room humming, the home fires burning, for putting up with my overuse of metaphors, for allowing me the space to do the work I love by taking on where my strengths and interests (hello spreadsheets!) most certainly don't lie. Special mention to one Julie Doyle, my business mentor who transformed my business through both her commercial expertise as well as her unwavering belief and support. More importantly, Julie's my friend who's always up for an adventure, knowing full well there'll be a couple of unplanned extra kilometres and snort-laughs aplenty.

My circle (s) of friends who make me laugh til I cry, let me cry then make me laugh. Our group chats are a sight to behold and here's hoping they're never made public. You know who you are.

My 'once upon a time': Mum, Dad and Saher, where my storytelling life began.

My 'and they lived happily ever after': Raphy-Joe for being my dream making, booty shaking, pizza baking, grass raking, chocolate taking husband. You're the rock behind everything here at Blue51 HQ and I couldn't be more grateful.

Finally, Gabriella and Alessia. Moxie indeed. Never let go of your moxie. I love you and live by your example.

About the Author

Holly Cardamone is a Melbourne-based writer, communications specialist and all-round Word Nerd who works with people to tell their story and grow their brand using beautiful communications.

Through her consultancy, Blue51 Communications, Holly provides strategic and specialist communications support and writing services. She writes anything and everything, almost always with a smile on her face, a coffee within grasp and a space-invading Australian Shepherd on her feet.

Holly earned her postgraduate Master of Arts (Communications) at Swinburne University, chased up by her Master of Arts (Professional Writing and Literature) at Deakin University.

A committed long-term niche-dodger, she has worked with businesses and organisations of all sizes and sectors to clarify their message and connect with their ideal clients, getting them the results they desire and deserve. She's down to earth, smart as a whip and funny to boot, with the ability to cut to the core of a story with practical, relevant and solutions-focused specialist advice and support.

Holly is wife to a devilishly handsome Carlton Football Club tragic, mama to two feisty cherubs and her favourite place is waterside. She's a lifelong language connoisseur, a mostly inconspicuous eavesdropper, a voracious reader, an almost fearless box jumper (Google it) and is hands down the person you want on your table at a trivia night.

www.ingramcontent.com/pod-product-compliance
Lightning Source LLC
Chambersburg PA
CBHW042121190326
41519CB00031B/7577